PETROC™
LEARNING RESOURCES

Please return this item on or before the last date shown below.

1 9 OCT 2010
1 0 JAN 2014

2 4 JAN 2014

WITHDRAWN FROM STOCK

1 9 JAN 2015
2 7 JUN 2016

The Library, Barnstaple Campus
Telephone: 01271 338170
Email: library@petroc.ac.uk

Liberalism

Modern Ideologies

LIBERALISM

D. J. Manning
Department of Politics,
University of Durham

LONDON
J. M. DENT & SONS LTD

Preface

This book is designed to present an understanding of liberalism from a combination of two distinct standpoints. The first surveys the ideological character of liberalism, and the second the character of liberalism as a particular ideology. The first approach deals with the form of ideological writing found in the work of liberal authors. The symbolism, vocabulary, logic and objectives of liberal political theory are examined, and the relationship between liberal theory and practice is discussed. This approach may be described as philosophical. The other is more historical. All but the last of the six chapters of the book also deal with the unique response of liberal authors to political events, changing social and economic conditions and the emergence of new intellectual climates. The questions asked here are: What is it that liberals believe, and how do they seek to justify the holding of these convictions? Together it is hoped that the two approaches provide a comprehensive survey of the status and range of the liberal tradition of ideological thought. However, one aspect of liberal ideology has been avoided, namely its subjectivity. This is a book about liberalism. It is not a liberal book. The advocation of the liberal point of view, no less than a critique of liberal values from a Marxist standpoint, is wholly incompatible with it. The author's claims are made on non-ideological grounds.

I record that some of the ideas advanced in this book were developed in the M.A. postgraduate seminars in politics at the University of Durham. I would like to thank Dr Gordon Graham in particular for the contribution he has made towards their formation. Responsibility for their failings is mine.

Durham, 1976   D. J. M.

Contents

For Harold and Helen

1 The Symbolic Form of Liberalism

The original implications of the term liberal, like the term imperialist, were, for the most part, derogatory. Liberals represented to the early nineteenth-century statesman a threat to the re-established order of post-Napoleonic Europe in the same way that, later, in the minds of the liberals themselves, the imperial ambitions of Napoleon III threatened the constitutional practice of republican France. Characteristically, in England, liberalism was at first regarded as a foreign disposition. The title liberal was used by the Tory minister Castlereagh in 1816 as a term of abuse, and when, in 1822, Byron, Shelley and Leigh Hunt founded a journal called *The Liberal* the venture proved to be no great success. It was not until 1879 that an English journal of that name was to flourish. By this time Gladstone's party, and the political opinions of many of Europe's most prominent political thinkers, Wilhelm von Humboldt, Benjamin Constant, Alexis de Tocqueville and John Stuart Mill amongst them, were styled liberal. At the end of the century this party and these opinions were associated with an intellectual tradition of great distinction. Writers of the calibre of Locke, Voltaire, Montesquieu and Adam Smith were elected ancestors of a teaching in a way comparable with the claim made by twentieth-century socialists with respect to Morelly, Charles Fourier and Henri de Saint-Simon. This is not to suggest that Locke, Voltaire, Montesquieu and Smith were, during their lifetime, known as liberal in any sense other than that they were of liberal education and inclination in the eighteenth-century meaning of the term. The first to be called liberals, or *liberales*, were members of the Spanish Cortes of 1810–11.

The intellectual ancestors of liberalism did not, like the classical economists and philosophical radicals, belong to a school. Their political opinions were various, and the subject and occasion of their writing disparate. Nevertheless, their being captured in the same retrospective vision was not a mistake. Although they had not elaborated one coherent doctrine, their opinions came to acquire a particular significance in the light of what self-conscious liberals said at a later date. Certainly this illumination is coloured by the preoccupations and prejudices of a later age. It picks out some, but not all, of the salient features of the work of those now claimed for liberalism. Nevertheless, there is continuity in the ancestral line in which the new-found fathers of liberalism had been given a place. The autobiography of liberalism, like that of J. S. Mill, may not meet the strict criteria of historical writing. The material is selected and ordered with a view to illuminating a subsequent, not a precedent, state of mind. In giving an account of their past, twentieth-century liberals have been inclined to make no more reference to Locke's views on salvation than did Mill to his anonymous attacks on Bentham's and his father's radicalism.[1] But the fact remains that the later outlook is more clearly characterized, if not explained, by this kind of writing with hindsight, and it was, of course, with a view to distinguishing the liberal tradition from that of rival ideologies that it was undertaken by sympathetic commentators like Leonard Hobhouse.[2]

Hobhouse's characterization of the liberal point of view is, in many respects, an admirable account, but it is drawn from inside rather than outside the liberal tradition. It is, in fact, a contribution to that tradition. The essence of liberalism for Hobhouse is a development of its most recent interpretation, which, in its orientation towards the social condition of late nineteenth-century England, is rather different from that which preceded and followed it. At any given time a retrospective vision of liberal writing from within the tradition tends to be biased by a preference for contemporary relevance, and whereas this is desirable from the point of view of its political significance, it is undesirable from that of academic objectivity.

Before attempting a characterization of the conceptual framework of ideological liberalism as a whole, in so far as this is possible, it is first of all necessary to define what is to be understood by liberalism as a tradition of ideological writing. Not only are there many political opinions which are not liberal, not all of the opinions of liberals are ideological. The systematic character of ideological argument, for example, makes it an inappropriate weapon in parliamentary debate. In modern democratic assemblies political arguments are too brief to be conclusive. The settlements at which parliamentarians arrive are reached according to constitutional convention rather than demonstrable reason. The members of parliamentary assemblies are prepared to abide by majority decisions with which they do not agree. As a Member of Parliament J. S. Mill was frequently obliged to comply with a ruling in favour of a proposal to which he had objected, but in his defence of representative government he could not be overruled, as distinct from countered by another argument. The ideological confrontations in which liberals engage are not at an end until one or other of the disputants is persuaded that he is mistaken in his view. The ideologist claims to stand outside the political arena on grounds of incontestable truth, although he wishes to influence the course of events within it. His theories are presented as an objective philosophical, historical or scientific account of human experience and his plans as to its improvement are based on first principles. His opponents stand accused of error. For example, liberal intellectuals engaged in ideological confrontation have, in Friedrich von Hayek's words, first to demonstrate that their philosophy alone is consistent with a 'true theory of human nature'.[3] Ideological arguments have more the character of a battle than a debate. Anyone can join in. The contributions are addressed to the public at large and appear in print rather than are heard by a group of privileged participants in the privacy of a meeting. From reading Mill's political works the public is left in little doubt as to where he stands in relation to life, and in this lies part of his achievement as an ideologist. Indeed, it is on account of their comprehensiveness and fundamentalism that we can derive a deeper understanding of liberalism as an ideology from the writings of Mill, de Tocqueville and

Hobhouse than we can glean from the political speeches of the liberal ministers Gladstone, Cavour and Thiers. However, it is not the case that we find a complete expression of liberalism in the works of any one writer or group of writers.

A tradition of ideological writing, of the kind of which liberalism is an example, cannot be said to have a particular point of origin in time, or to culminate in a single work. Liberalism was, in its various aspects, an attitude of mind before it became a self-conscious theoretical exposition. Seen in total its history reveals many deviations and transitions. For example, the importance Locke ascribes to natural law, J. S. Mill to utilitarianism and T. H. Green to moral self-realization prevents the integration of their work into one coherent doctrine at their own level of abstraction. A tradition of political thought does not possess the coherence of a systematic piece of theorizing in spite of the fact that any one such work is best understood in the context of the tradition to which it belongs.

The relationship between a tradition and individual contributions to it is obviously important to the understanding of both. Each may be seen as exercising a formative influence on the understanding of the other, although the two are distinct. To talk about one liberal writer is to say something about liberalism as a whole, and to talk about liberalism should inform us of some characteristics common to individual writers in this class. It is less clear how the common element in the relationship between the individual contributions to an ideology, which are themselves abstract, can be demonstrated. We cannot take a writer like Locke, who did not call himself a liberal ,and present him as the archetypal representative of the tradition, on the evidence of his own arguments, without indicating the sense in which these arguments are liberal. It will not do to maintain with John Plamenatz that Locke is a liberal just because he uses arguments subsequently employed by men who were known as liberals in the nineteenth century.[4] If liberalism is to be characterized it has to be established where the underlying unity of thought amongst all those now called liberal lies, otherwise we will be obliged to define liberals as Lockeans or the disciples of some other major theorist. The trouble with this claim is that it is circular. It excludes the possibility of our accepting that those called liberals, who do not follow Locke or some other author directly, are *bona fide* members of the tradition. There is even an objection to maintaining that every genuine liberal work has a Lockean, or some other, element in it. It is that an ideology has in each expression to be sufficiently systematic in its exposition to appear to prove a political conviction correct. It cannot be a random collection of arguments. What we can say is that Locke's political theory is one of the faces that liberalism can pull, and occasionally does. It is compatible with its bone structure. But it is not an appearance that liberalism has always presented or must again present to retain its identity. The identity of liberalism is to be found in the limits of its transfigurations, not in the persistence of a collection of individual expressions.

Liberalism, then, is a tradition of ideological writing. Its ideological character can be discerned in a variety of individual works noted for their fundamentalism and systematic argument in favour of the destruction, preservation or reform of this or that institution or practice. At the same time, although there are persistent themes in the tradition, the works it has inspired present a variety of programmes and principles which bear no obvious relationship to one another outside the context of an historical development. It simply will not do to attempt to characterize liberalism by taking the work of Locke, Mill or Green as representing the essential teaching of the tradition, or by concentrating only on the development of those points of view in vogue amongst those at present regarded as its principal representatives. To illuminate the liberal vision of society it is necessary to demonstrate how its many manifestations are related to a common framework of thought which does not support contributions to other traditions of ideological writing. In short, we must characterize the tradition as a whole. It is proposed that the following three principles serve this purpose: the principle of balance, the principle of spontaneous generation and circulation, and the principle of uniformity. These principles are not presented as unstated assumptions of liberal arguments. They are presented as expressed features of liberal thinking.

The Balanced Society

For the liberal, the world of human affairs may be seen to be in a stable state provided that no social, economic or political imbalance be allowed to develop. It has frequently been observed that, in its earlier phases, liberalism treats the individual as prior to society as an historical being or philosophical concept. Many liberals assert that society is not more than the sum total of its members whose rights or interests its institutions are properly concerned to protect. It is claimed that it does not evolve over time. It is presented as a static set of relationships. In later liberal thought the subservience of society to man is a muted theme, and the idea that it does not evolve is no longer heard. However, one point constantly recurs in each and every manifestation of liberal thinking. It is the belief that the liberty and welfare of the individual and the justice and security of society depend upon there being clearly defined and enforced legal relationships between all of its members. No man may rightly be considered outside or above the law.

Social and political relationships for the liberal are artificial. They are rational constructs designed to counter such imperfection otherwise inevitably experienced by men competing for wealth and position whilst valuing privacy and leisure. A system of law is the liberal solution to the predicament of the civilian entrepreneur whose search to improve his own economic and social position encourages others to covet his achievements. Liberalism, as a teaching deeply attached to stability and freedom, emphasizes the importance of rules and obligations in all voluntary associations. Their purpose is to preserve the opportunity for every individual to join with others in rewarding relationships not injurious to others. A marriage, a church, a business and a political party are, for liberals, necessarily rule-bound associations which all civilians have a right to enter and an obligation to respect. According to Locke's contribution to liberalism civil society is itself just such an association. It originates in a voluntary agreement to live according to rules which preserve the opportunity to enter relationships of one's choice while protecting one from being coerced into serving others. For Locke the greatest threat to human liberty took the form of violence to property and persons. Consequently, 'in all the states of created beings capable of Laws, where there is no law, there is no Freedom. For Liberty is to be free from restraint and violence from others which cannot be, where there is no Law.'[5]

The liberty that the nineteenth-century liberal believed his intellectual ancestors to have secured for the citizen, indeed, the liberty that made a man a citizen, is liberty defined in law. Liberty is the creation of legal restraint. It is to be found where restraint is justly imposed on government by constitutional law, and on the private citizen by civil and criminal law. Together they prevent the arbitrary interference of one man in the affairs of another. Liberty thus understood is not a power over others—the liberty to do as one wills without fear of retaliation—the power of a master over his slave. It is security from interference which makes a man free. It is for this reason that freedom is closely related to private property in liberal thinking. Moreover, because the right to property is a universal right, in the same sense that freedom is a universal right, no man can properly have property in another man. Slavery denies the humanity of both the slave owner and the slave. For any one member of society to enjoy the freedom created by legal security it has to be guaranteed for all, and to this end the state must possess sufficient coercive force to punish any individual who violates the rights of others. To determine when such a violation had occurred and by whom, be it private individual or public agent, a judicial system independent of political and private influence must be established. According to Locke it could never have been the intention of people to 'put a force into the Magistrate's hand to execute his unlimited Will arbitrarily upon them: This were to put themselves into a worse condition than the state of Nature . . .'[6] The purpose served by law is the prevention of the abuse of power. From Locke and Montesquieu to Lord Acton and Sir Ernest Barker the liberal mind has insisted that power corrupts because 'every man invested with power is apt to abuse it, and to carry his authority as far as it will go . . . To prevent this abuse, it is necessary from the very nature of things

15

that power should be a check to power.'[7] At every level in society 'the liberty of each is thus relative to that of others, and has to be adjusted to that of others, it must always be regulated; and indeed it would not exist unless it were regulated'.[8]

Liberal arguments in favour of a separation or division of power between the executive, legislative and judicial branches of government are not different in purpose from those which advocate the legal restraint of monopolistic capitalism and stress the danger inherent in popular opinion and mass movements. There is a curious symmetry about the remarks of Locke, Madison and Montesquieu on government, Smith, William Graham Sumner and Hayek on private enterprise and free competition and Mill, de Tocqueville and Ortega y Gasset on the intolerance of the masses. They represent in America, England and continental Europe an adherence to a political, economic and social Newtonianism in which the stability and movement of society depend upon its constituent parts remaining in balanced relationships. Excessive accumulations of power, wealth or opinion are direct threats to society's dynamism and equilibrium. A liberal society is a pluralistic society precisely because the concept of countervailance is essential to its understanding of liberty, and liberty is the first concern of the liberal.

The Motivation of Man

One of the beauties of the Newtonian universe is the fact that it is self-moving and eternal in its motion. The society characterized in liberal ideology is also a perpetual-motion machine. It generates within itself its own inexhaustible energy in the form of the human will which, directed along the path of reason, sustains the order necessary for the stability and survival of society. For liberals compulsion is undesirable because the motive force of society and the energy for social reform originate in the spontaneity of the independent mind and the power of the liberated will. It was for this reason that Mill and von Humboldt feared the possibility that state-controlled education might impose dull uniformity and mediocrity on the young. State education might achieve a degree of social tranquillity, but, as von Humboldt pointed out, 'such an artificial equilibrium ... leads to sterility or lack of energy; while on the other hand, the pursuit of particular objects which is characteristic of private education, produces an equilibrium more surely without sacrifice of energy, through a variety of relationships'.[9]

The liberal is apt to underpin all obligations with moral obligation since it is the moral will which generates the power which sustains all human relationships. It is inconceivable that we could properly or successfully be compelled by the state to perform the obligations prescribed by natural law, the principle of utility or idealist ethics. Liberals tell us that it is the motive power of the moral will that effectively sustains society, not the coercive power of society that efficiently moves the vast majority of men to comply with its ethical and legal rules. As T. H. Green pointed out, paternalism is misguided:

> The real function of government being to maintain conditions of life in which morality shall be possible, and morality consisting in the disinterested performance of self-imposed duties, paternal government does its best to make it impossible by narrowing the room for the self-imposition of duties and for the play of disinterested motives.[10]

The consequences of such an unnatural impediment to human development are inescapable. A repressive society, we are told, is necessarily hierarchic and reactionary, and it is therefore prone to revolutionary overthrow. The generation of essential energy at first stagnates and then, as a result of its circulation being constricted, fails to sustain the basic functions of government. The result is collapse. A stable society is essentially a free society. It requires free speech, free press and free association in order that it be obliged to respond to the needs and ideas of its members. Governments must respect the autonomy of the individual in order that it be able to perform its own functions. The evil that liberals have perceived in slavery, child labour, assembly-line production, lack of educational opportunity and the exploitation of colonial people is one which originates in treating human beings as means to an end rather than as ends in themselves. Without this basic consideration they cannot achieve creative self-determination and moral responsibility, and, hence, their society is deprived of its motive power, and man of the possibility of progress. In this spirit Hobhouse wrote:

> The heart of Liberalism is the understanding that progress is not a matter of mechanical contrivance, but of liberation of living spiritual energy. Good mechanism is that which provides the channels wherein such energy can flow unimpeded, unobstructed by its own exuberance of output, vivifying the social structure, expanding and ennobling the life of mind.[11]

In the nineteenth century the threat to the creativity of the individual was not, of course, confined to repressive régimes. Individualism and the energy it generates were threatened by the tyranny of social conformism. As Mill was quick to point out:

> Protection, therefore, against the tyranny of the magistrate is not enough: there needs protection also against the tyranny of the prevailing opinion and feeling; against the tendency of society to impose, by other means than civil penalties, its own ideas and practices as rules of conduct on those who dissent from them; to fetter the development, and, if possible, prevent the formation of any individuality not in harmony with its ways, and compels all characters to fashion themselves upon the model of its own.[12]

The emergence of the European urban poor and the world's multitudes later addressed by modern means of communication fostered this liberal fear of the conforming masses. It was of the crowd in the French Revolution that Constant wrote:

> The crowd, corrupted by both the danger and example, tremulously repeated the slogan required of them, and took fright at the sound of their own voice. Everyone formed part of the multitude, and was afraid of the multitude he helped to enlarge. It was then that there spread over France

the unaccountable lightheadedness which has been called the reign of terror.[13]

It was to the phenomenon of mass man that the Spaniard Ortega y Gasset attributed the rise of totalitarianism. 'Liberalism,' he wrote, '. . . it is well to recall this today—is the supreme form of generosity; it is the right by which the majority concedes to minorities and hence it is the noblest cry that has ever resounded in this planet.' Alas, at the time of writing, he was obliged to observe:

> Nothing indicates more clearly the characteristic of the day than the fact that there are so few countries where opposition exists. In almost all, a homogeneous man, weighs on public authority and crashes down, annihilates every opposing group. The mass—who would credit it as one sees its compact, multitudinous appearance?—does not wish to share life with those who are not of it. It has a deadly hatred of all that is not itself.[14]

In the liberal tradition a parallel relationship exists between motivation and stability in politics and motivation and stability in economics. In both there exists an emphasis on individualism and freedom of action. In man's economic life it is, of course, self-interest, rather than self-imposed moral responsibility, which moves the mechanism of the market. In the pursuit of material gain man's limited ability, and limited concern for the welfare of others, precludes the possibility of his directly advancing the fortune of any but himself and his dependants. However, given that the condition of open competition is maintained, the energy he expends creates opportunities for others. The mechanism of the market itself directs labour and capital towards the creation of the maximum of desirable products at the lowest cost.

According to liberal economists from Smith to Hayek the weighty interference of the state in the creation and distribution of wealth is likely, for reasons of selfishness and ignorance, to result in misappropriation and inefficiency. This, in turn, discourages the initiative and sacrifice which motivates the economy as a whole.

There has inevitably been considerable conflict of opinion amongst liberal economists and moralists as to the rôle of the state in regulating the terms of economic competition. This has, however, for the most part involved the issue of equality of opportunity rather than the principle of competition. The ortho-dox view remained that without competition the resources of society simply will not gravitate to the time and place at which their utility can be maximized. In the later nineteenth century the controversy centred on the importance to liberty of freedom of contract. The opinion which prevailed was that of Green:

> To uphold the sanctity of contracts is doubtless a prime business of government, but it is no less its business to pro-vide against those contracts being made, which, from the helplessness of one of the parties to them, instead of being a security for freedom, become an instrument of disguised oppression.[15]

This conclusion, through the work of John Dewey, became known in America. Far from creating opportunity for all, an unregulated freedom of contract, like any other unregulated freedom, leads to despotism. Men cannot compete unless they are in a position to do so. The destruction of mercantilism, the control of corporate capitalism and resistance to the nationaliza-tion of industry, like the destruction of aristocratic patronage and the restraint of the masses, are, we are told, essential to the dynamism of a free society.

The laissez-faire economy of liberal theory presupposes that all are able to compete on equal terms, just as the liberal view of parliamentary government presupposed that all can actively participate in public life. The recognition, in the face of the nineteenth-century polarization of classes and mass parties, that neither was the case led to the formulation of a programme de-signed to help those who could not compete and participate. This development added the doctrine that the only acceptable basis for the receipt of public health, welfare and education is need, to the accepted belief that the only proper basis for public employ-ment is ability. However, in liberal theory the regulation of the life of the individual with a view to securing him a place in society has always been counterbalanced by the fear that this regulation encourages dependency on the part of the citizen and dictatorial tendencies in public administration. This has been particularly noticeable in America where attempts by government agencies to assist ethnic minorities have been deeply resented by some liberals. The use of force to achieve racial integration through the desegregation of schools has divided the liberal conscience against itself.

From the liberal point of view there is no way in which the human condition can be radically altered through an organized attack on imperfection. Man will never be eternally freed from the corruption of power, the exploitation of the weak and the tyranny of ignorance by resort to government oppression or revolutionary purge. The fight against deprivation and moral turpitude is the responsibility of every individual, and any attempt to transform the self-moving society into the directed society must necessarily destroy the harmony and balance of its rational order. Liberals believe that progress has been and will continue to be made in the quality of human life, but, from the liberal point of view, all such progress will be piecemeal and gradual. Moreover, it will originate in the form of individual contributions to the great debate on man's condition conducted in free and liberal institutions. It will not stem from the dictates of the masters and servants of a corporate state standing apart from a subject body and claiming possession of some hidden truth.

According to J. S. Mill there exists 'a twofold division of the merit which any set of political institutions can possess. It consists partly of the degree in which they promote the general mental advancement of the community . . . and partly of the degree of perfection with which they organize the moral, intellectual, and active worth already existing, so as to operate with the greatest effect in public affairs.' [16] Having adopted this classification, he found that there is 'no difficulty in showing that the ideally best form of government is that in which sovereignty, or supreme controlling power in the last resort, is vested in the entire aggregate of the community; every citizen not only having a voice in the exercise of that ultimate sovereignty, but being, at least occasionally, called upon to take an actual part in the government by the personal discharge of some public function, local or general.' [17]

Representative government is good government because it is balanced and progressive. Liberal arguments concerning political change stress the importance of gradualness; a course steered between the dangers of reactionary neglect, leading to anarchy, and revolutionary transformation, leading to totalitarian dictatorship. The guarantee of progressive government is the participation of an educated public and the accountability of all who hold public office. A government unresponsive to the needs of the governed must necessarily encourage social disintegration and political unrest. Misgovernment is accompanied by the tendency of individuals to 'drop out' of society, minorities to break away from the state, majorities to attempt to overthrow it unless intimidated by force, and the destruction of society by civil war. In the liberal hypothesis, the withdrawal from society, of the kind common amongst the young and idealistic in America of the 1950s and '60s, the foundation of separatist movements, such as those of the Irish and Basque nationalists, the organization of mass revolution, successful in France and Russia and the experience of civil war suffered in America and Spain are all deemed to be the consequence of the arrest of the internal cyclical motion of the body politic. They constitute a breakdown in communication and co-ordination. They are perverse manifestations of society's motive power no longer harnessed for the common good within a rational system of law. Montesquieu's expression of the principle is representative:

> What is called unity in a body politic is a very delicately balanced thing; true unity is unity or harmony which results in all the parties, no matter how opposed they may seem to be, working for the general good of the society just as discords in music work for the whole harmony . . . It is like the parts of the universe which are eternally linked by the action of some and the reaction of others.[18]

In short the principle of balance is closely related to the principle of the generation and circulation of society's motive power. The Italian liberal Guido de Ruggiero, in his study of the history of European liberal politics, expressed this understanding in the following way:

> A liberal government . . . allows the conflicting opinions and interests to check and balance each other, the forces of Society to reach a state of equilibrium, and this, working with a material already of itself reduced to equilibrium, without the intervention of the government, imparts movement to the whole with a minimum expenditure of energy on the part of the state.[19]

The Realization of Universal Order

So far it has been suggested that two principles, which gave unity to Newtonian cosmology, are to be found at work in liberal thinking about man and society. In their liberal context they are, that the stability of society, like the stability of the universe, depends upon the maintenance of the relationships between its parts, and that the energy required to sustain the harmony of these relationships originates within the system as a whole in a manner comparable with that controlling the order and movement of the planets. It remains to put forward a third principle common to the form of the Newtonian and liberal visions. This is the principle that we may expect democratic institutions to materialize in human societies whenever they reach the appropriate level of development, just as we might expect any physical phenomenon to materialize given the presence of the sufficient condition for its occurrence. The principle holds considerable fascination for liberal political scientists for obvious reasons. As the American Seymour Martin Lipset put it in explaining the purpose of his book *Political Man*:

> This book's concern with making explicit the condition of democratic order reflects my perhaps over-rationalistic belief that a further understanding of the various conditions

under which democracy has existed may help men to develop it where it does not now exist.[20]

Liberals believe that human nature is universally the same, and that differences of race, nationality, sex, class and religion do not mask significant differences in intelligence and emotional disposition which would preclude the possibility of the formation of a civil society and representative government. Uncivilized behaviour within an underdeveloped country, like uncivilized behaviour in industrial countries, is attributed to adverse conditions, such as poverty. Tribal and feudal societies represent steps in the formation of civil society, which alone possesses the energy and stability to sustain the promise of a high level of material and spiritual wellbeing for all of its members. Mill devoted a good deal of time to elaborating the principle:

> The state of different communities, in point of culture and development, ranges downward to a condition very little above the highest of the beasts . . . A community can only be developed out of one of these states into a higher by a concourse of influences, among the principal of which is the government to which they are subject . . . and the one indispensable merit of a government, in favour of which it may be forgiven almost any amount of other demerit compatible with progress, is that its operation on the people is favourable, or not unfavourable, to the next step which it is necessary for them to take in order to raise themselves to a higher level.[21]

In order that a government be able to meet this requirement it is necessary that it be in the hands of the most energetic and informed class of its time. During his own lifetime Mill considered this to be the middle class. The aristocracy had been seduced by 'lazy enjoyment. In the same ratio in which they have advanced in humanity and refinement, they have fallen off in energy and intellect and strength of will.' [22] For their part, the working class was as yet unprepared for political responsibility. Indeed 'no lover of improvement can desire that the predominant power should be turned over to persons in the mental and moral condition of the English working classes . . .' [23] For Mill the future of civilization lay with education in the widest sense. It was education which would break down the restrictive barriers of class and increase the possibility of further progress. In de Tocqueville's view the destruction of caste and class was necessary for the dissemination of the very idea of progress. The American experience suggested to him that:

> In proportion as castes disappear and the classes of society approximate—as manners, customs, and laws vary, from the tumultuous intercourse of men,—as new facts arise,—as new truths are brought to light,—as ancient opinions are dissipated, and others take their place,—the image of an ideal but always fugitive perfection presents itself to the human mind. [24]

For the liberal, progress and freedom are inseparable ideas. The only real measure of progress is in fact freedom, and by freedom is meant the development of the responsible and autonomous self. In Green's words:

> When we measure the progress of a society by its growth in freedom, we measure the progress . . . by the greater power on the part of the citizens as a body to make the best of themselves. [25]

Only a free society can generate the intellectual and moral energy to increase its own resources.

The constitution of the Newtonian universe is one of elements possessing irreducible mass moved through Euclidian geometric space by a force independent of the passage of time. It has existed in this its present state since the creation. Indeed it is the creation itself, and within it the laws of its motion have universal application. It is the very permanence of the universe that has made it the ideal measure of human time. The cyclical motion of the earth measures out the history of human consciousness in a perfectly symmetrical chronology. And, to the extent that man's institutions achieved a comparable stability and harmonious function their history is progressive. Without the vision of the universe as a perpetual-motion machine, and the ideal of human institutions organized on similar principles, the liberal concept of progress is inconceivable. They bring together the idea of duration and the idea of perfection suggesting that man's history had a goal which only perverse stupidity could thwart.

It was against this cosmology that Darwin's evolutionary theory struck a blow. Darwin's work suggested that temporal events were without a goal. Existing organisms had evolved by a process of natural selection simply because they had proved better able to adapt themselves to arbitrary change. Within evolutionary time many forms of life had appeared and disappeared, and the existence of man was but a relatively recent occurrence with no special guarantee of permanence. The prestige of the Newtonian vision was to suffer a further eclipse with the advent of Einstein's work which challenged the finality of Newtonianism as a framework for scientific research and understanding. And the work of the theoretical scientists Kurt Gödel, Alan Turing and Alfred Tarski has led to the surprising conclusion that:

> An axiomatic system cannot be made to generate a description of the world which matches it fully, point for point; either at some points there will be holes which cannot be filled in by deduction, or at other points two opposite deductions will turn up. And when a contradiction does turn up, the system becomes capable of proving anything, and no longer distinguishes true from false. That is, only an axiom which introduces a contradiction can make a system complete, and in doing so makes it completely useless.[26]

The implication of this conclusion is that the possibility of science discovering an ultimate and comprehensive set of axioms from which all natural phenomena can be shown to follow by deductive steps does not exist. This development in the philosophy of science has been followed by another in the history of science. This is Thomas Kuhn's thesis concerning the generation of scientific knowledge. It suggests that far from working towards a single general theory embracing all natural phenomena, scientists have been engaged in the establishment and overthrow of paradigms within which a limited number of puzzles concerning the relationship between an hypothesis and observations can be solved. To the extent that these theories become necessarily more complex, and the technology of their verification more sophisticated, the more inflexible they are in the face of further theoretical innovation. However, they are not immune to overthrow, and when such a paradigm of 'normal science' is dethroned Kuhn calls the event a revolution. In doing so he is fully aware of the image of political experience this evokes.

> Political revolutions are inaugurated by a growing sense, often restricted to a segment of the political community, that existing institutions have ceased adequately to meet the problems posed by an environment that they have in part created. In much the same way, scientific revolutions are inaugurated by a growing sense, again restricted to a narrow subdivision of the scientific community, that an existing paradigm has ceased to function adequately in the exploration of an aspect of nature to which that paradigm itself had previously led the way. In both political and scientific development the sense of malfunction that can lead to crisis is prerequisite to revolution.[27]

In science, as in politics, we can expect only the fittest to survive, and by fittest Kuhn does not mean the ultimate best, only the best in the light of recent information or circumstances. These conditions may be said to improve or deteriorate only in the context of the established framework of understanding. The scientist no longer entertains the view that the Newtonian universe is a fixture. Its order is but a period in the history of stellar evolution and the Newtonian conception of it is not part of a final theory of all natural phenomena.

What, if anything, does this imply for liberalism in so far as it has a symbolic form similar to that of Newtonianism? Could it be that recent developments in the history and philosophy of science manifest an alternative form? What is more to the point, could it be the case that this alternative form is shared with a political

27

doctrine opposed to liberalism; for example, revolutionary socialism?

Now it is a characteristic of revolutionary socialism that it conceives the political order, not normally in a stable state, but rather as evolving through a series of radical transformations commensurate with revolutions in human consciousness. The doctrine suggests that man's cultural experience is an historical process. In it, it is impossible to engineer the retention of an outmoded form of public order once the circumstances in which it was established have been transformed. In ripe circumstances a revolution creates its own consciousness, and in pre-revolutionary circumstances it is impossible to have more than a vague idea what form this will take. To date, in the West, liberalism has, for the most part, successfully resisted the attractions of revolutionary socialism. It has been particularly successful in resisting the appeal of perpetual revolution, but it could be that the strength it formerly derived from the Newtonian cosmology may, in the future, turn into a weakness.

From the dawn of man's theoretical defence of political structures there has existed in his mind a relationship between the political and cosmological order. It finds expression in the Platonic and Thomist traditions, and liberalism is no exception. Whether or not the political is to be understood as a microcosm of the cosmic order, or the cosmic as the macrocosm of the political, is of little importance here. What is important is the fact that the vision of either one has lost substantial appeal when its similitude has been successfully challenged by a rival. Now it is not suggested that those who adhere to the Kuhnian view of science are supporters of revolutionary socialism. The history and philosophy of science are not ideologies, but ideology does require the appearance of some historical, philosophical or scientific substantiation to lay claim to the kind of certainty the ideologist believes men require to act with confidence in the modern world. To secure this it must be possible to draw convincing analogies between the academic discipline and ideology in question. If this cannot be done the ideology cannot usefully be claimed to be true in the relevant academic sense. It is, therefore, conceivable that a diminution in the popular belief in the finality of Newtonian science could affect the appeal of liberalism, as we now understand it, to future generations. If this does occur it would be surprising if liberalism did not modify its symbolic form. There is nothing which is indispensable to a tradition of ideological thought. Its symbolic form, theoretical foundations, principles of political practice and policy recommendations may all be changed. Ideologies are not characterized by an unchanging essence. The symbolic form of liberalism outlined in this first chapter is not advanced as the criterion by which genuine liberal principles or policies can be distinguished from others erroneously associated with this ideology by its adherents. It is not brought to the liberal tradition as an *a priori* construct. There is no alternative to accepting that liberalism is all that has been recognized as authentic by men of reputation who have professed sympathy with its varied aspirations. It just happens to be the case that liberalism has the symbolic form of Newtonian science. Admittedly, the three features of the form do not all enjoy the same degree of prominence in every work claimed for liberalism, but they are never altogether absent. Where we find that one of them has been replaced by an alien feature, rather than neglected, this is related to a liberal reaction to the intrusion. For example, Rousseau's rejection, rather than neglect, of the aspect of balance can be detected in his identification of the moral, or real, will of the individual with the political, or general, will of the whole community. Rousseau does not recognize a need to preserve, in political society, the autonomy which he ascribes to man in a state of nature. In granting man one liberal condition of moral life—society—he takes away another—freedom. He does not erect legal barriers between citizens, and between them and their government. There is no case for the strict separation of public from private life in his ideal republic. For this assertion he is, amongst others, condemned by J. S. Mill, Benjamin Constant, Sir Henry Maine, Sir Isaiah Berlin and Jacob Talmon as an enemy of liberalism. In a very different way, Jeremy Bentham too gave offence in this respect. The sovereignty he conferred on the interest of the majority violated the same notion of limit, or the aspect of balance, that Rousseau has rejected. He was condemned for this by J. S. Mill, Francis Montague, Sir Henry Maine, T. H. Green, Lord Lindsay and Sir Ernest Barker. Rousseau and Bentham have, of course, been admired by men with a liberal reputation. It is not true that everything that they wrote is alien to liberalism. However, although Kant had a high opinion of Rousseau, and Mill respected Bentham, it was not liberalism that Kant detected in Rousseau and Mill in Bentham. Rather, it was the raising of what they considered to be major issues in moral and legal philosophy.

2 Liberty and the Liberal Tradition of Discourse

A picture taking the form of three persistent features of liberal thinking has been outlined and an attempt made to show that, in spite of the originality of successive liberal writers, their ideas not only may be, but are, located within this landscape. The symbolic form of liberalism is not the metaphysical foundation upon which the ideology has been progressively built and to which liberals can refer those who doubt the soundness of the construction. It merely frames the world-view of liberals, enabling, but not obliging, those who have accepted it as part of their cultural heritage to support a variety of policies determined in the context of changing circumstances. Little more is claimed for this symbolic form than its persistent appearance in the writings of recognized liberals and their intellectual ancestors. Although it is called Newtonian it is not suggested that Newton's work did more than encourage its appreciation. The form probably had as much to do with the popularity of Newtonian science as had that corpus of knowledge to do with the appeal of the symbolic form. The form is not itself a scientific hypothesis. Its appeal is aesthetic rather than scientific.

The history of liberalism cannot be portrayed successfully as the progressive completion of a list of consistent policies. There does not exist at any one time a complete programme supported then, and thereafter, for the same reasons by all who are called liberals. Changing intellectual climates and historical circumstances have led each major contributor to the liberal tradition to complete his work uninhibited by the prescriptions of earlier writers. It is tempting to consider mid-nineteenth century liberal theories and prescriptions as representing the doctrine in its maturity. This would, were it possible, enable us to search for the originators of each of its conclusions and the last to subscribe to them. But the search for the essential liberal programme, like the search for its unique metaphysical foundation, is doomed to failure. In the case of liberalism both policies and theoretical foundations constantly change.

There is, however, more to be said about the development of liberalism than that it has a persistent symbolic form. The symbolic form of liberalism is little more than a map of the geography of the ideology. There is also its biography. In seeking to illuminate the development of liberalism it is possible to detect the formation and exploration of the application of a set of arguments. Arguments may, on occasions, prove irrelevant, but they need not be abandoned. Unlike a refuted theory, and a policy that has been effected, a flexible argument can be called upon again and again. An argument can be compatible with a particular principle without being inseparable from it. The same argument can, over time, be used to support a variety of different policies. Of course, the arguments most favoured by liberals are not necessarily the most telling they have used in any one debate, and they may be borrowed by ideologists of a different persuasion prepared to risk the charge of ideological impurity. Moreover, that certain arguments are important to any account of liberalism does not imply that liberals have employed them on every occasion on which they might have been used. However, it is proposed to show that, in the case of the arguments for toleration, they had, for a considerable period of time prior to the nineteenth century, been used by men whose names have been associated with liberalism, and that in Mill's work they developed along identifiable lines. There is nothing anarchic about a tradition of discourse, and this is one of the things that an ideology is.

The search for the historical origins of arguments now identified as an integral part of liberal rhetoric, and the attempt to trace their incorporation in this ideology, is a difficult undertaking. Arguments for liberty, particularly religious, intellectual and moral freedom, which are the subject of this chapter, are not only to be found in works written before the arguments were adopted by men known as liberals, they are found in the company of reasoning which liberals have found unconvincing. Certainly, the main arguments J. S. Mill elaborated in his essay *On Liberty* are not his own invention. For the most part they originally appeared in seventeenth-century religious and philosophical works which made, at best, an indirect contribution to the rise of liberalism. They were later taken up by eighteenth-century Whigs and radicals anxious to determine the boundary between public and private concerns in a civil society. Not until the nineteenth century were they used by recognized liberals to justify reforms calculated to safeguard and encourage the progress of civilization.

It is here proposed to trace the ancestry of Mill's arguments, not with a view to diminishing Mill's achievement, but to follow the exploration of the potential in a set of ideas. Just as the painter of an abstract picture begins with tentative imagery, and proceeds to explore and elaborate its aesthetic implications, so the contributors to the liberal tradition may be seen as developing a series of arguments out of unrelated reactions to events. As we follow the formation of the series we witness the emergence of a tradition of discourse—a way of talking politics from a particular point of view. With the passage of time this tradition is increasingly capable of authenticating fresh inspiration within the expanding limits of its total intelligibility. At the same time those who contribute to the tradition become increasingly conscious of doing so.

In the case of Milton's *Areopagitica*, Locke's *Letter Concerning Toleration* and Mill's essay *On Liberty* we have individual masterpieces of liberal writing. No one of these works exhausts the inspiration the tradition affords, but each is, in its own way, a more comprehensive treatment of the subject than we find in earlier writing admired by recognized liberals. A living tradition is sustained, not exhausted, by its new creations. At the same time, each masterpiece, although not a final statement, is a complete one. The above-mentioned works are each more than a characteristic expression of the symbolic form of liberalism. And each is more than a set of additional points. All are systematic arguments—works of striking vigour—as much masterpieces on account of what they ignore as on account of what is central to their illuminating power.

The telling of the story of the origin, adoption and development of the liberal idea of freedom requires a criterion of selection, chronological succession and reference to changing historical circumstances. All the writers selected not only used arguments which progressively became the heritage of liberal intellectuals, they have all been revered by nineteenth-century liberal writers, or their recognized precursors. The date of publication of each of the works to which reference is to be made is given to establish the temporal relationship between them, and a brief outline of the occasion of their publication is provided where it helps to illuminate their original force. For the purpose of comparison many of the arguments are quoted at length.

The Appeal to Conscience

In Europe, extended arguments for religious toleration and freedom of learning were first heard during the Reformation and Renaissance. Neither event was concerned with the creation of the civil society admired by liberals. They brought to European politics theocracy and autocracy rather than the concept of civil rights. Moreover, many of the greatest intellectual masterpieces of the period, Calvin's *Institutes of the Christian Religion* and Hobbes's *Leviathan* amongst them, are taken by liberals to be authoritarian, in spite of the fact that in them are to be found the seeds of a new and radical individualism.

The story of the struggle for freedom of conscience and intellectual freedom may begin with the reaction of two great Catholic humanists, More and Erasmus, to the initial stages of the Reformation. Both were sympathetic to the Protestant reformers, in so far as they too were critical of the corruption at Rome, but both feared for the unity and humanity of the Church in the coming struggle between the supporters of doctrinal reform and orthodoxy. In his *Utopia*, published in 1515, More outlined what he understood to be the Christian position on theological controversy. Ideally it 'should be lawful for every man to favour and follow what religion he would, and that he might do the best he could to bring others to his opinion, so that he did it peaceably, gently, quietly and soberly, without lusty and contentious rebuking and inveighing against others'.[1] More's arguments for religious toleration, if not quite fresh from the mint, had many years of wear in them before they were withdrawn from circulation. They are that any conviction short of atheism should be tolerated, firstly, in order to avoid 'dissension amongst the people', secondly, because it is an 'arrogant presumption to compel all other by violence and threatenings to agree to the same that thou believest to be true', and thirdly, because 'the truth of its own power would at the last issue out and come to light'.[2] Some ten years later Erasmus reflecting sadly on the intensifying conflict between Rome and Luther observed: 'On the one side we have Bulls, edicts and menaces: on the other revolutionary pamphlets which set the world in flames.'[3] In spite of his sympathy for Luther's revulsion for the avarice of the mother church he could not, on the one hand, approve of the spirit of enthusiasm in which Luther's attack on Rome was conducted. On the other, while desiring Christian unity, he had 'small belief in submission extorted by Bulls and Imperial edicts. They may claim the tongues of men: they cannot touch their minds.'[4]

The developments of arguments for religious toleration received considerable impetus from the death of Michael Servetus in 1553. As the authority of Rome was progressively challenged, religious persecution became increasingly common, but the fate of Servetus was unusual in that he was burnt by a Protestant council at Geneva, and solely for the publication of his theological opinions in his *Christianismi Restitutio* of 1552. He was not engaged in the subversion of all institutional authority as were the Anabaptists. There is no direct attack on the political order in his work, and in so far as his views might be judged offensive they were more likely to give offence to the Catholic than the Protestant Church. Servetus was burnt at Calvin's instigation simply for views at variance with those to be found in the *Institutes*. The action proved divisive for the reformers. In 1554 Calvin felt obliged to publish *Defensio Orthodoxae Fidei*, a defence of the

35

forceful suppression of heresy, but the work did not stem the growing tide of criticism of the part he had played in the trial of Servetus.

In the same year that Calvin had published his *Defensio*, Castellion of Basle published his *De Haereticis*. In this he strongly objected to the punishment of Servetus, and in his following work, *Contra Libellum Calvini*, he severely criticized Calvin's *Defensio*. It seemed ridiculous to Castellion to presume that theological issues disputed for centuries could now be settled by force. The belief was not only contrary to reason: it was contrary to the explicit command in the Bible that every Christian should love his fellow men. If Servetus was in error then this should have been demonstrated, but to burn him for his sincere conviction, alone by which he could attain salvation, was not only contrary to revealed religion, it was unlikely to achieve its objective if this be religious conformity. The death of a man for his convictions testified to the strength of his faith, not that of his persecutors. Calvin's disciple, Théodore de Beza, replied on behalf of his master in his own *De Haereticis* of 1554. Castellion, he informs his readers, has cast doubt on the very possibility of determining true faith and misconstrued the duty of the civil magistrate. The purpose of political society is not the mere provision of peace and security. It is the creation of the circumstances in which men can serve God. It cannot therefore be a matter of indifference to the civil magistrate what perverse interpretation be put on scripture. Heresy is necessarily a subversion of political order.

As the Reformation and counter-Reformation took their course, religious and political duties became increasingly fused for both Protestant and Catholic alike. The consequence of the view that a challenge to religious orthodoxy entailed a challenge to political authority was to promote the most intense conflict wherever religion divided the population of a state. France had to endure thirty years of religious war before the attempt to impose religious uniformity was first abandoned. Even then, for Calvinists and Catholics, the issue was not resolved. Between the claim that the tenets of the Christian faith were plainly set out in the scriptures for all men, and the claim that Rome was privileged with the duty of conveying true Christianity there was no basis for a compromise. Acontius, a disciple of Castellion, altogether failed to convert the Christian protagonists to toleration with the argument of his *Strategematum Satanae* of 1565. He maintained that it was ridiculous to suppose that truth could be established by force, or by the weight of opinion, and that it was ridiculous to believe the civil magistrate competent, or any church sufficiently impartial, to judge disputed matters of faith. Free inquiry and discussion alone could illuminate the Christian teaching. The imposition of any one interpretation merely encouraged hypocrisy amongst those obliged to make an outward show of accepting the teaching of an established church. The arguments already appear familiar.

The first works sensitive to the reappearance of religious toleration after the initial impact of the Reformation and counter-Reformation appeared in England and Holland. Richard Hooker, Hobbes and Spinoza insisted upon the supremacy of political over ecclesiastical authority in matters relating to religious practice while arguing in favour of freedom for the Christian conscience. For them the threat to religious liberty came not from civil authority. It came from religious fanatics. In his *Of the Laws of Ecclesiastical Polity*, the first four books of which were published in 1594, Hooker affirms that there is no 'law of Christ's which forbiddeth kings and rulers of the earth to have ... sovereign and supreme power in the making of laws, either civil or ecclesiastical'. It is left to 'the world's free choice' who shall exercise the power of making law and in England that power 'resteth in the person of the king'.[5] For Hobbes, whose *Leviathan* was published in 1651, it was indisputable that Christian sovereigns 'have all manner of power over their subjects, that can be given to man, for the government of men's external actions, both in policy and religion ... for both State and Church are the same men'.[6] And for Spinoza, whose *Tractatus Theologico-Politicus* was published in 1670, even 'the rites of religion and the outward observances of piety should be in accordance with the public peace and well-being, and should therefore be determined by the sovereign power alone'.[7] Nevertheless, Spinoza was equally insistent that it

37

is not the 'object of government to change men from rational beings into beasts or puppets, but to enable them to develop their minds and bodies in security . . . In fact, the true aim of government is Liberty.'[8] It is, he tells us, 'an abuse of sovereignty and a usurpation of the rights of subjects to seek to prescribe what shall be accepted as true, or rejected as false, or what opinions should actuate men in their worship of God'.[9] Hobbes also had recognized that the sovereign cannot command or forbid faith, 'because belief and unbelief never follow men's commands. Faith is a gift of God, which man can neither give, nor take away by promise of rewards, or menaces of torture.'[10] The sovereign may command adherence to an interpretation of scripture and this command must, in all outward appearances, be obeyed, but 'profession with the tongue is but an external thing, and no more than any other gesture whereby we signify our obedience . . .'[11]

To meet the claim of the religious enthusiast that his faith authorizes the imposition of his beliefs on others by force, Hooker, Hobbes and Spinoza made a distinction between religious faith and practice. Faith is a matter of reason and revelation, only practice falls under the jurisdiction of law. Faith is a matter between man and God. It is from the human point of view self-regarding, but practice is a matter affecting other men. It is other-regarding, and necessarily the concern of the sovereign whose principal object it is to preserve public peace and security.

Milton, in his *A Treatise of Civil Power in Ecclesiastical Causes shewing that it is not Lawful for any Power on Earth to Compel in Matter of Religion*, published in 1659, found it necessary to ask the following of his fellow Protestants living under the rule of a Protestant sovereign:

> If then we count it so ignorant and irreligious in the papist, to think himself discharged in God's account, believing only as the Church believes, how much greater condemnation will it be to the protestant his condemner, to think himself justified, believing as the state believes?[12]

Milton was prepared to tolerate the Catholic faith, but not the Catholic Church, which is an institution 'supported mainly by a civil, and except in Rome, by a foreign power: justly therefore to be suspected, not tolerated by the magistrate of another country'.[13]

Christ has decreed that the 'inward man' can never be reached by force of arms, only by divine grace. Force can only control outward behaviour, and, whilst this is adequate for securing compliance with human law, it is totally inadequate for securing obedience to God. In England, at a time when it pleased God that the church and state be married, it was legitimate for the magistrate, with divine guidance, to impose conformity, but since God has seen fit to separate church and state what 'was then a lawful conjunction, to such on either side as join again what He hath severed would be nothing now but their own presumptuous fornication'.[14] Bearing this conviction the Pilgrim Fathers had left for America in 1620.

With Milton the claim, but not the principal argument, for religious toleration has moved on from that of Hooker, Hobbes and Spinoza. It is now affirmed that the Protestant church is independent of the state in matters of religious practice as well as faith. Indeed, the state not only has no right to interfere in matters of faith and modes of Protestant worship, every citizen has a duty to resist such interference. There is a further development in Milton's treatment of the subject of religious toleration. Hooker, Hobbes and Spinoza had, from experience, reason not to encourage open debate on religious issues. Milton saw reason to encourage it. He extends the argument for toleration of belief and worship to defend the discussion and publication of religious opinions. In so doing he aligned himself with Castellion and Acontius, who, unlike Hooker, Hobbes and Spinoza, feared the exercise of political authority in religious affairs no less than the violent disputing of sects. However, the distinction between the autonomous inward man and the man whose outward behaviour is subject to law is common to all their writing, and, in the work of Locke, to whom it then passed, it served as the basic premise of all four major arguments for religious toleration in what must be regarded as one of the definitive statements of the principle.

Locke published a number of papers on the subject of tolera-

Liberalism

tion. The most famous, *A Letter Concerning Toleration*, appeared in Holland and England in 1689. It is strictly Protestant in spirit, reflecting his sympathy for the Arminian Remonstrants. Locke's first argument for toleration is seemingly directed against Catholicism. The authoritative source of Christian inspiration, he tells us, is the Bible, on a reading of which it is plainly evident that 'no man can be a Christian without charity, and without that faith which works, not by force, but by love'.[15] In Locke's opinion a man who attempts to impose his personal interpretation of Christianity by force necessarily contravenes the revealed will of God. It God had intended to convert by force how much easier it would be 'for him to do it with armies of heavenly legions, than for any son of the church, how potent soever, with all his dragoons'.[16] He has not chosen to use force, and so it is evident that compulsion and conviction are incompatible in matters of faith. In his first argument for toleration Locke has appealed to Protestant theology and then common sense.

Locke's second argument makes more explicit the distinction he has already employed between spiritual and temporal affairs. It is used to determine the character of a true church. The care of men's souls, he tells us, is altogether different from the preservation of life, liberty, health, leisure and worldly possessions. The former may be secured by 'inward persuasion' only, the latter by 'outward force'. Sincere conviction can alone secure salvation. Faith cannot be guaranteed by compulsion. At best force can only secure the outward signs of conformity, and to procure such hypocrisy is in itself an offence against God.

> All the life and power of true religion consists in the inward and full persuasion of the mind . . . to whatever outward workings we conform, if we are not fully satisfied in our own mind that the one is true, and the other well pleasing unto God, such profession and such practice, far from being any furtherance, are indeed great obstacles to our salvation.[17]

Locke is utterly uncompromising on this point. 'I may grow rich,' he wrote, 'by an art that I take no delight in, I may be cured of some disease by remedies that I have not faith in; but I cannot be saved by a religion that I distrust, and by a worship that I abhor.' [18] In matters of religion, reason and conscience are sovereign, and it follows that a church can be nothing other than 'a voluntary society of men, joining themselves together of their own accord in order to the public worshipping of God in such a manner as they judge acceptable to him, and effectual to the salvation of their souls'.[19]

Locke's third argument deals with the claim of a church to have the right to discipline its own members and to interfere in the affairs of another congregation. He took the view that beyond demonstrable reason and revelation there is no ground for the conviction that a faith is orthodox. As a free association of men of common conviction no church can impose a teaching on grounds of its theologians claiming that they are specially privileged with the truth. Apparently with the Catholic Church in mind, Locke suggests that those who claim that their ecclesiastical authority is derived directly from the apostles produce 'the edict by which Christ has imposed that law upon his Church' [20] (a useful but dangerous argument for a contractual theorist). No church has a right to persecute. It certainly has the right to excommunicate any one of its members when exhortation, admonition and advice fail, but 'excommunication neither does, nor can, deprive the excommunicated person of any of those civil goods that he formerly possessed. All those things belong to the civil government, and are under the magistrate's protection.' [21] In his third argument for toleration Locke has, therefore, used the distinction between civil and religious associations he expanded in the second argument to justify the subjection of all churches to the authority of reason and revelation in spiritual matters and to the rule of law in non-spiritual affairs. He has also found fault with the Catholic claim to orthodoxy on grounds of the lack of historical evidence that it was commissioned by the apostles to spread the Christian faith.

Locke's fourth argument for toleration concerns the promotion of good conduct and truth. 'Covetousness, uncharitableness, idleness, and many other things are sins, by the consent of men, which yet no man ever said were to be punished by the magistrate. The reason is, because they are not prejudicial to other men's rights, nor do they break the public peace of societies.' [22] Similarly 'the magistrate ought not to forbid the preaching or professing of any speculative opinions in any church, because they have no manner of relation to the civil rights of the subjects'.[23] Truth like morality 'is not taught by laws, nor has she any need of force to procure her entrance into the minds of men. Errors indeed prevail by the assistances of foreign and borrowed succours. But if truth makes not her way into the understanding by her own light, she will be but the weaker for any borrowed force violence can add to her'. [24] Where beliefs lead to practices unlawful 'in the ordinary course of life', such as the sacrifice of infants, they may not be tolerated in a religious meeting. Moreover, those whose religion prepares them 'upon any occasion to seize the government, and possess themselves of the estates and fortunes of their fellow-subjects' are no more to be tolerated than those atheists, who, having no faith in God at all, are utterly unrestrained by the 'promises, covenants and oaths' upon which civil society is founded.[25] Only law-abiding and God-fearing men are entitled to the respect of the magistrate. It is the magistrate's unwarranted invasion of their privacy that justifies resistance. In this, his closing argument, Locke employs the distinction he has made between matters to be determined by reason and revelation, and matters to be determined by law, to specify who is and who is not entitled to toleration. In so doing he introduces an element of prudential reasoning into his argument. There are classes of actions and belief that must be suppressed at all cost, and others against which the use of force is not only undesirable, but ineffectual and potentially dangerous to the magistrate himself.

Locke's *Second Treatise of Government* by chance provided a convenient defence of the revolution of 1688, but *A Letter Concerning Toleration* could not be used, as had Hooker's *Laws*, to justify the establishment of the Church of England. Locke did, in fact, find himself assailed by the defenders of establishment. It was some years before a thorough revision of Hooker's position on the relationship between toleration and establishment appeared. This is to be found in William Paley's *The Principles of Moral and Political Philosophy*, published in 1785. In this work utilitarian considerations, which had a very shadowy existence in Locke's work, are made the principal justification for the control of religious practice by law. 'There is nothing,' Paley informs us, 'in the nature of religion, as such, which exempts it from the authority of the legislator, when the safety or welfare of the community requires his interpretation.' [26] Certainly, 'acts of the legislature . . . cannot affect my salvation . . . but they may deprive me of liberty, of property, even of life itself, on account of my religion . . . because the property, the liberty, and the life of the subject, may be taken away by the authority of the laws, for any reason which, in the judgment of the legislature, renders such a measure necessary to the common welfare'.[27] Paley's position is quite different from Locke's on the issue of civil rights. However, it is far from Paley's purpose to advocate religious persecution. It is, he believed, desirable that all religious beliefs which do not threaten public peace and welfare be tolerated, because 'every species of intolerance . . . is adverse to the progress of truth . . . Truth results from discussion and from controversy; [it] is investigated by the labours and researches of private persons . . . In religion, as in other subjects, truth, if left to itself, will almost always obtain the ascendancy.' [28] Paley was convinced that if a perfectly free dialogue were allowed between Catholics and Protestants the Catholic faith would reform itself along Protestant lines.

The Appeal to Reason

So far we have traced in barest outline the development of a number of related arguments for religious toleration. These survived the period of their formation, and, along with arguments for freedom of secular learning and publication, they were later used to counter new and previously unimagined threats to liberty. It is to the arguments for freedom of secular learning and publication that we now turn. In so doing we encounter the spirit of scepticism.

Now the development of European scepticism was not a disposition entirely compatible with the spirit of Protestant individualism. To the extent that scepticism encouraged the growth of scientific understanding it was acceptable, but where it furthered radical philosophical and historical criticism of revealed religion it could not be embraced by Protestant writers. Before the most radical arguments deployed by the sceptics could be employed by Protestant liberals the metaphysical foundation of liberalism had to be moved from Christian to utilitarian grounds. If we compare Locke's reflections on the reasonableness of Christianity with Hume's on miracles it is apparent that Hume's scepticism has led him to conclusions unacceptable to Locke. The tradition to which Bayle, Fontenelle, Hume, Helvetius and d'Holbach belong encouraged more than an attack on the Catholic Church and an attempt to distinguish the original text of the Bible from inauthentic additions. It was not inspired by the religious passion of Erasmus, Milton and Locke, rather it could, and did, in the case of Hume, Helvetius and d'Holbach, lead to near if not absolute atheism. Extreme sceptics conceived morality as independent of religion, and supported a purely secular view of politics entirely foreign to the notions of natural law and revealed truth essential to the arguments of Erasmus, Milton and Locke. In short, scepticism and materialism had no historical affinity with the politics of liberalism. In his political thinking Hume was conservative and Helvetius and d'Holbach were radicals. Voltaire, who is claimed for liberalism, did derive considerable inspiration from the anti-clericalism of Bayle and Fontenelle, and from the doubt that their historical research threw on the credibility of miraculous Christianity. But for Voltaire the deist this attack on dogmatic religion merely cleared the way for empiricist philosophy and experimental science, and the great leaders in this field he believed to be Locke and Newton, neither of whom had any major quarrel with their own clergy and both of whom found the Bible a valuable source of religious inspiration.

The new spirit in philosophy and science, in a diluted form, far from eroding religious faith provided it with fresh support. For Voltaire, Locke and Newton the perception of a rational order in the universe suggested that it must be the work of a rational and all-powerful creator. Scepticism also encouraged the development of the historical consciousness. But here again, it is the scepticism of men critical of human institutions, particularly the Catholic Church, not the existence of God. It is the scepticism of Voltaire, d'Alembert and Gibbon, not Hume, Helvetius and d'Holbach, which contributed to the growth of the Whig and liberal interpretation of the past later expounded by Henry Hallam, Lord Macaulay and Lord Acton.

The first plea for freedom of secular learning and inquiry was made by Bacon and Descartes with a view to freeing science and philosophy from the confines of the scholastic tradition. It did not involve a direct attack on established religious belief and practice. Both took care not to offend religious authorities. Bacon's views on religious toleration are very similar to those of Hooker, and Descartes went so far as respectfully to delay the publication of his arguments supporting a theory for which Galileo had been condemned by the Catholic Church. In his *Novum Organum* published in 1620, Bacon identifies the enemies of the new learning as men whose uncritical admiration for classical and mediaeval authors prevented their appreciating experimental science. Sadly he found that 'in the customs and institutions of schools, academies, colleges, and similar bodies destined for the abode of learned men and the cultivation of learning, everything is found adverse to the progress of science'.[29] Quite wrongly science has been categorized as a form of learning dangerous to religion when it is in fact her handmaid 'since the one displays the will of God, the other his power'.[30] Descartes's *Discourse on Method*, published in 1637, may be considered the rationalist counterpart to the *Novum Organum*. Inspired by the conviction that the foundations of scholastic philosophy were unsound, he sought to make a new beginning by refusing to accept anything that cannot be shown to be the case. If others were to follow his example Descartes believed it possible that each could build on the achievements of his predecessors. As man's knowledge increased by this method it seemed equally reasonable to expect that the practical application of discoveries would 'render ourselves the lords and possessors of nature'.[31] With this conclusion Bacon heartily agreed. The idea of progress and the principle of freedom of inquiry were closely related from the beginning of the seven-teenth century. Unless men are free to follow the dictates of reason we cannot, Spinoza tells us, expect 'progress in science and the liberal arts: for no man follows such pursuits to advantage unless his judgment be entirely free and unhampered'.[32]

In Milton's *Areopagitica: A Speech for the Liberty of Un-licenced Printing*, published in 1644, the arguments for freedom of conscience are brought together with those for freedom of learning and the freedom of the press. According to Milton the pursuit of virtue, like the pursuit of truth, will prove successful only when it involves rational understanding. Behaviour originat-ing in blind conformity to authoritative direction or custom is no better than the acceptance of truths without an understanding of the reasoning which distinguishes them from falsehood. To be able to identify virtue and truth men must know vice and false-hood. They cannot become good and wise from being protected by the magistrate from evil and ignorance. 'Since, therefore, the knowledge and survey of vice in this world is so necessary to the constituting of human virtue, and the scanning of errors to the confirmation of truth, how,' asks Milton, 'can we move safely, and with less danger, out into the regions of sin and falsity, than by reading all manner of tractates, and hearing all manner of reasons?'[33] It is, in fact, presumptuous of the magistrate to attempt to guard the individual from vice and ignorance, which God has admitted to the world in order that men may more surely know virtue and truth. With precision Milton informs us that 'God sure esteems the growth and completing of one virtuous person, more than the restraint of ten vicious'.[34] It is in any case quite futile to attempt to propagate virtue and truth by authority. 'A man may be a heretic in the truth; and if he believes things only because his pastor says so, or the assembly so determines, without knowing other reasons, though his belief be true, yet the very truth he holds becomes his heresy.'[35] Liberty not authority is the friend of truth. 'Let her and falsehood grapple; who ever knew truth put to worse, in a free and open encounter?'[36] Of course, by virtue and truth Milton understood Protestant virtue and truth. It is inconceivable for Milton that liberty of opinion

46

might allow men to abandon Protestantism for Catholicism or atheism. For many this belief was convenient rather than convincing, but, in England, it became increasingly acceptable that toleration was no threat to virtue, truth or peace. This was not the case in Catholic Europe.

Within the jurisdiction of Rome the belief prevailed that the imposition of conformity was essential. Almost a hundred years after the appearance of Milton's *Areopagitica* Voltaire had still to argue, in his *Treatise on Toleration* of 1763, that 'candour and toleration have never excited civil commotions; while intolerance has covered the earth with carnage'.[37] Far from public discussion and rational argument provoking civil disorder it was the organized attempt to suppress it that gave rise to conflict. 'Who are they,' he asked, 'who have brought the flame of discord into their country? Was it Pompanacius, Montague, le Verger, Descartes, Gassendi, Bayle, Spinoza, Hobbes, Lord Shaftesbury. . . ? By no means: they were generally theologians, who being at first actuated with the ambition of becoming head of sects, had soon afterwards adopted that of being chiefs of a party.'[38] When we 'consider that Newton, Locke, Clarke and Leibniz, would have been persecuted in France, imprisoned at Rome and burnt at Lisbon, what are we to think of human reason?'[39] With Bacon and Descartes 'reason began to make some small progress in the world, and to penetrate the fogs and darkness of the schools, as well as to thin the mazes of popular prejudices'.[40] The result is the achievements of Locke and Newton. Voltaire helped to transform the spirit of seventeenth-century scepticism into that of eighteenth-century rationalism from which liberalism was to derive a large part of its optimistic faith in progress. He was assisted by Helvetius.

In his treatise *On the Mind*, published, and then banned by both religious and civil authorities, in 1758, Helvetius affirmed that all opinion ought to be tolerated, except opinion intolerant of the different belief of others. Upon the free exchange of opinion depended the growth of human knowledge. In his treatise *On Man* he claimed that: 'If Descartes, Corneille, Etc. rendered the reign of Louis XIII illustrious; Racine, Bayle, Etc. that of Louis

XIV, Voltaire, Montesquieu, Fontenelle, Etc. that of Louis XV it is, because the arts and sciences were under these different reigns, successively protected by Richelieu, Colbert, and the late Duke of Orleans the regent.' [41]

Condorcet, whose *Sketch of a Historical Picture of the Progress of the Human Mind* appeared in 1773, agreed. Dividing history into ten stages Condorcet portrayed man's advance from barbarism to civilization in terms of the discovery and the victory of truth over error. In the ninth stage, which commenced with Descartes's attack on scholasticism, and in which Condorcet believed himself to be living, science was to triumph over dogmatic religion preparing the way for universal brotherhood and material well-being.

Across the Channel a similar faith in the power of reason and the potential of science is to be found in William Godwin's *Enquiry Concerning Political Justice*, first published in 1793. 'The direct tendency of science', Godwin informs us, 'is to increase from age to age, and to proceed, from the slenderest beginnings, to the most admirable conclusions.' [42] 'Truth and falsehood cannot subsist together: he that sees the merits of a case in all clearness, cannot in that instance be the dupe either of prejudice or superstition.' [43] It was believed that one of the consequences of the emergence of truth and justice was an egalitarian society in which each would have sufficient for his basic needs. The enthusiasm of Condorcet and Godwin was deemed sufficiently contagious for Thomas Malthus to feel obliged to direct his harshest criticisms against their teaching in his essay *On the Principle of Population*, published in 1798. He argued that attempts to improve the material condition of human life by redistributing wealth were doomed to failure. Only the limiting of the size of the population was compatible with the fact that man's material resources, particularly that of food, were limited. Malthus's essay was to have a major impact on the course of liberal thinking. It dampened the spirit of optimism that had grown to replace that of scepticism, and it prepared the ground for the reception of an altogether more tough-minded doctrine—the doctrine of the survival of the fittest associated with the name of Herbert

Spencer. The immediate background to J. S. Mill's classic
presentation of the arguments for liberty, however, is the
philosophical radicalism of Jeremy Bentham and James Mill, not
the pessimism of Malthus. Bentham and James Mill owed little to
Godwin and Condorcet. They also rejected the natural-law
tradition and the contractual theory of government. They were,
as everyone knows, utilitarians and materialists, closer to Helvetius and d'Holbach than to Locke and Voltaire. Empiricist
philosophy and Newtonian science they embraced, but in their
elaboration of a science of government the tradition of Protestant
individualism and Enlightenment deism is replaced by the more
radical individualism and the materialism of the pleasure-pursuing
and pain-fleeing man. The Benthamite man possesses autonomous
reason, interest and will, but he does not have an inviolable
conscience. The liberty Bentham and Mill considered appropriate
for social man was the liberty to pursue unrestrained his private
interest provided that, as a member of a minority, he did not
invade the privilege of having the largest share of the cake
properly enjoyed by the majority. Unfortunately the social
organization necessary for such co-ordination had nowhere been
established. Ignorance on the part of the people, and sinister
interest on the part of their rulers, had resulted in an irrational
political order in which the greatest happiness of the greatest
number went unrealized. The happiness of the many was sacri-
ficed for that of the privileged few. The task of political science
was to redeem this situation by education and reform. The difficulties were many, but not insuperable. For such is the power of
man's reason that 'when all the evidences are equally presented to
his observation, and equally attended to, to believe or disbelieve
is no longer in his power. It [the belief] is the necessary result of
the preponderance of the evidence on one side or the other.' [44]

In securing responsible government Bentham and James Mill
considered that the liberty of the press was essential. Only when
the people are properly informed as to the actions of their representatives, and the representatives thereby obliged to follow the
wishes of the people, may we expect responsible and informed
government. It is evident, argued James Mill, that 'there is no

safety to the people in allowing any body to choose opinions for them; that there are no marks by which it can be decided before-hand, what opinions are true and what are false ...' However, we may be assured that if 'all opinions, both true and false, are equally declared, the assent of the greater number, when their interests are not opposed to them, may always be expected to be given to the true'.[45]

The Status of Mill's Essay 'On Liberty'

John Stuart Mill's essay *On Liberty* was published in 1859, by which time religious conflict occasioned by the Reformation was an exhausted passion. In England the passage of the bill for Catholic emancipation of 1829 still left Jews and atheists subject to legal discrimination, but this intolerance did not amount to persecution. The 1832 Reform Bill had achieved, in the minds of most liberals, the degree of representative and responsible govern-ment appropriate to the political maturity of the populus. The older universities were emerging from their eighteenth-century slumber and new ones were being established. Far from being the centre of resistance to intellectual adventure they were increas-ingly the home of its inspiration. Mill was one of the last major English political theorists not to hold a chair in one of them. Equally important, newspapers were free to report the nation's affairs and few works of intellectual merit were subject to censor-ship. In movements of this kind England undoubtedly led the world, but in Europe as a whole, and in America, similar develop-ments were under way. The old enemies of liberty were on the retreat. However, instead of universal freedom new threats to liberty had made their appearance. One at least, Mill observed, had been encouraged by the very success of the reformers. Where they had formerly sought to check the power of government, by constitutional procedures and parliamentary institutions, they had more recently advocated that the people direct its use. The power of popular government had been represented as 'the nation's own power, concentrated, and in a form convenient for exercise'.[46] 'This mode of thought, or rather perhaps of

feeling,' Mill regretted, 'was common amongst the last generation of European liberalism, and in the continental section of
which it still apparently predominates.' [55] It had not been appreciated that the will of a majority can be every bit as despotic as that
of a minority. More formidable still was the tyranny of society
over the individual. His moral and intellectual autonomy was
now in urgent need of a defence against the 'tyranny of the prevailing opinion and feeling; against the tendency of society to
impose, by other means than civil penalties, its own ideas and
practices as rules of conduct on those who dissent from
them . . .' [48] Finally there was the threat of the bureaucratic state
which, 'instead of calling forth the activity and powers of
individuals and bodies, [it] substitutes its own activity for theirs;
when, instead of informing, advising, and, upon occasions,
denouncing, it makes them work in fetters, or bids them stand
aside and does their work instead of them'. [49] As Mill perceived
the situation, the dangers of religious fanaticism, arbitrary
government, reactionary scholarship and official censorship had
been supplanted by new evils, the roots of which were to be found
in majoritarian radicalism, the increase in the uneducated and
conforming urban population and the expanding functions of the
state.

In the face of these new and formidable threats to liberty it was
apparent that the freedom of the individual had yet to be ade-
quately defended. Only in the case of the campaign for religious
liberty do we find that 'the rights of the individual against society
have been asserted on broad grounds of principle, and the claim of
society to exercise authority over dissentients openly contro-
verted'. [50] What was required was a more comprehensive defence
applicable to all situations and societies bar those in which the
backwardness of the people obliges us to exercise the same
paternal authority we are obliged to exercise over children. Mill
defined the freedom he had in mind as follows:

> It comprises, first, the inward domain of consciousness,
> demanding liberty of conscience in the most comprehensive
> sense; liberty of thought and feeling; absolute freedom of

opinion and sentiment on all subjects, practical or speculative, scientific, moral, or theological. The liberty of express-
ing and publishing opinions . . . Secondly, the principle
requires liberty of tastes and pursuits, of framing the plan of
our life to suit our own character; of doing as we like,
subject to such consequences as may follow: without
impediment from our fellow-creatures, so long as what we
do does not harm them, even though they should think our
conduct foolish, perverse, or wrong. Thirdly, from this
liberty of each individual, follows the liberty, within the
same limits, of combination among individuals; freedom to
unite for any purpose not involving harm to others: the
persons combining being supposed to be of full age, and not
forced or deceived.[51]

To establish this liberty Mill advanced three major arguments.
The first calculated to resist the dictatorial tendencies of the
political will of the majority and the private will of the intolerant
and anti-social person. The second to resist the oppressive conformity of mass society, and the third to resist the diminution of
the sphere of individual initiative in human affairs by the bureaucratic state.

The first argument is drawn from the contribution to the liberal
tradition made by the great system builders of the sixteenth and
seventeenth centuries. It is founded on a distinction between those
actions which threaten the interests, liberty and peace of others
and those which can harm no other than their author. The distinction served to authorize the exercise of sovereign authority to regulate human relationships whilst denying it the right to direct human
actions. In a famous passage Mill tells us that 'the sole end for
which mankind are warranted, individually or collectively, in
interfering with the liberty of action of any of their number, is
self-protection. That the only purpose for which power can be
rightfully exercised over any member of a civilized community,
against his will, is to prevent harm to others. His own good,
either physical or moral, is not a sufficient warrant . . . over
himself, over his own body and mind, the individual is sove-

reign.' [52] It is only when a man's actions impose upon others that they ought to be subject to restraint. The business of law is to create the framework within which the individual is free. The attempt forcibly to oblige a man to follow a teaching or pursue a goal considered to be beneficial to him, no less than his being imprisoned or physically injured, is a violation of his liberty. In a manner similar to Locke, Mill argues that the business of government is the formation and enforcement of rules regulating social relationships and protecting the autonomy of the individual. At this point we observe the belief adopted by eighteenth-century Whigs, that liberty consists in the right to believe what one will and pursue goals of one's choice not injurious to others, being assimilated into utilitarian liberalism at the expense of Benthamite majoritarianism and Rousseau's idea of the general will.

Mills' second thesis has its roots in the Protestant doctrine of conscience and the Enlightenment belief in progress. It is this:

> If all mankind minus one were of one opinion, and only one person were of the contrary opinion, mankind would be no more justified in silencing that one person than he, if he had the power, would be justified in silencing mankind.[53]

In support of the principle are two familiar arguments: the first, that a received or imposed opinion, even if it be true, is of uncertain value when the grounds for holding it to be true are not understood; the second, that in suppressing any one opinion the whole of mankind either runs the risk of being deprived of intellectual advance or the confirmation of the superiority of an established belief. The only sure way we can guarantee the advancement and consolidation of learning is to allow every idea publicly to stand on its merits in order that it be subject to critical examination by all. 'Wrong opinions and practices,' Mill believed, must 'gradually yield to fact and argument—but fact and argument, to produce any effect on the mind, must be brought before it.' [54] 'If ever the Newtonian philosophy were not permitted to be questioned, mankind could not feel as complete assurance of its truth as they now do.' [55] If the truth of which we are most certain 'is not fully, frequently, and fearlessly discussed, it will be held as a dead dogma, not a living truth'.[56] And, truth 'thus held, is but one superstition the more, accidentally clinging to the words which enunciate a truth'.[57] Truth can be suppressed. Men can be obliged to recant true beliefs and profess false ones, but the cost in terms of moral and intellectual progress cannot be compensated for by any peace that conformity might temporarily secure. The suppression of the exercise of any man's critical and creative powers is an offence against the whole of humanity.

This second argument leads to Mill's third main proposition: namely, that unprincipled conformity diminishes man's capacity for moral action and constructive enterprise. 'The human faculties of perception, judgment, discriminative feeling, mental activity and even moral preference are,' he believed, 'exercised only in making a choice. He who does anything because it is the custom makes no choice. The mental and moral, like the muscular powers, are improved only by being used.' [58] It follows that those whose opinions are received, and whose behaviour is purely conventional, are liable to render their intellectual powers weak and their 'feelings and character inert and torpid, instead of active and energetic'.[59] Mill concludes his essay by arguing that a state which tries to monopolize the control of human affairs likewise prevents the generation of energy by its subjects, and thereby diminishes the possibility of achievement. The final words of *On Liberty* are:

> The worth of a state, in the long run, is the worth of the individuals composing it . . . a state which dwarfs its men, in order that they may be more docile instruments in its hands even for beneficial purposes—will find that with small men no great thing can really be accomplished; and that the perfection of machinery to which it has sacrificed everything will in the end avail it nothing, for want of the vital power which, in order that the machine might work more smoothly, it has preferred to banish.[60]

Man's right to liberty Mill founded on the principle of utility. 'I regard utility,' he wrote, 'as the ultimate appeal on all ethical questions . . .'; only on the widest applications of the principle of utility can we base an adequate defence of 'the permanent interests of a man as a progressive being'.[61] Mill has no place for revelation, salvation or natural law in his defence of liberty. He does not claim that man has a natural right to liberty. However, although his liberalism rests upon a different metaphysical foundation to that of the Protestants amongst his intellectual ancestors, some of the arguments he uses to defend liberty are a development of theirs. In *On Liberty* Mill brings the Protestant argument for the inviolability of conscience and the Whig argument establishing the bounds of private right and public authority together with the Renaissance argument concerning the danger of accepting authoritative opinion and the Enlightenment argument linking freedom to progress. His essay represents the consummation of the marriage, after a long engagement, of an unlikely pair.

In a book entitled *Liberty*, published in 1930, Everett Dean Martin lamented the ill-preparation of America's liberal youth to defend the values in which they believed against corruption, materialism and intolerance. He found it 'ironical that in a "free country" where public education is maintained at great cost, to prepare our youth to live in a nation dedicated to liberty, so little concern has been given to the understanding of liberty that great classics on the subject, like Milton's *Areopagitica*, Locke's essay on Toleration, and Mill's essay on Liberty—documents which should and could be known and understood by every high school student—are almost never taught'.[62] Martin's view of a liberal education may be defective, but his selection of texts is judicious. It consists of three of the greatest masterpieces in the history of liberal ideology. In comparison the works of Voltaire, Helvetius, Godwin, Paley and Bentham are merely links in the story. We cannot grasp the continuity in the development of the language of liberalism without referring to them, but they are only minor explorations of its potential. They also serve as links in the story of other articulations of human experience. Of the three essays selected by Martin it can be said that each, in its own way, is wholly permeated by the spirit of liberalism. Each is a complete exposition of an aspect of the liberal vision expressed in the language of a distinct tradition of discourse. No one of them

55

possesses the essence of liberalism as a whole. Each marks the culmination of a development, but no one of them eliminated the possibilities of the ideology finding further realms of expression. After Mill, for example, the idea of freedom was fruitfully explored again by T. H. Green.

We may say that the arguments of liberalism constitute the language of a tradition, because there is a sense in which they are learnt, not as a set of propositions, but as a medium of communication. Mill does not simply repeat the arguments of Milton and Locke. He applies, develops and transforms them. He introduces elements from other sources. He addresses the arguments to new problems, and he gives them an edge of his own. And yet Mill could not have done without his intellectual ancestors. He could not have invented his essay out of the blue. His inspiration has arisen in a definite context. The liberal tradition of political discourse is quite inimitable; no more to be copied than readily cast aside by those educated in its nuances. It is a facet of consciousness, something like style, but more formative, perpetually creative and yet perceptively a characteristic expression. The language of liberal discourse does not lend itself to the articulation of any point of view. Its authentic voice is a familiar utterance. It requires only a basic education in political thought to identify the voice of liberalism in any great debate. The language of liberalism has no single point of origin in history. It is native to the politics of Western Europe and of those countries strongly influenced by European culture, particularly America, but it did not issue from an event. For centuries it has existed in transmission, and still exists as an inexhaustible source of inspiration. When an occasion for a new birth presents itself those whose liberal education is complete may be relied upon to extend its life.

3 The Unity of Liberal Ideology

Many have regarded England as the home of authentic liberalism and suggested that where it has been expounded abroad it has either been exported there by Englishmen or imported by Anglophiles. The contribution to European and American political thought by writers with the reputation of Locke, Smith, Mill and Spencer, and the admiration of English political practice expressed by Voltaire, Montesquieu, de Lolme, Madame de Staël and de Tocqueville indicates the strength of the evidence supporting the claim that liberalism is an English tradition, or a reflection on English experience. But to admit that liberalism has deep roots in England's past does not, on the one hand, preclude the recognition of original contributions to the formation of this doctrine made by independent Continental and American writers, and, on the other, it does not entail the view that English liberalism is one thing and that native French, German and American liberalism are others. Nevertheless, Maurice Cranston has made this latter claim. He asserts that to 'write about liberalism in more than a domestic context one must write about liberalisms'.[1]

Cranston's argument is that although all liberals believe that the proper end of political activity is the realization of freedom they do not all subscribe to the same freedoms, and it is the kind of freedom to which they subscribe that determines what kind of liberals they are. We are informed that, in England, the character of native liberalism has been determined by the belief that freedom is 'freedom from the constraints of the state'. Cranston admits that this kind of liberalism has been professed in France, but he claims that it was advanced in opposition to the indigenous variety in which freedom is understood, not as freedom from state regulation, but as freedom to participate in the determination of national affairs. It was this latter kind of liberalism which came, in the German principalities, to supplant the English kind, which had found adherents in cosmopolitan circles prior to Napoleon's invasion. According to Cranston, nationalism amongst Germans became after 1812 'the very essence of their liberalism'[2] and remained so until 1918, since which time 'the old Lockean liberalism has twice been revived'.[3] Cranston believes that, in America, liberalism has been successively identified with the freedom associated with democratic government, unbridled capitalism and utopian socialism. At no point does he distinguish between the ideological writings of professed liberals and the activity of men whose political practice he chooses to call liberal, but in so far as he is clearly talking about political theories, he is of the opinion that there are several kinds of liberalism. He finds that those who have defined it as one doctrine have inevitably ignored those aspects of its teaching that their stipulative definition arbitrarily excludes. In order consistently to apply a coherent definition of liberalism they have had to select one kind of liberalism—English liberalism—and call this genuine liberalism, and treat every other kind as a perversion. This is certainly a mistake.

Cranston is doubtless right in maintaining that there are variants within the liberal tradition, but it is doubtful that their demarcations coincide with national boundaries, and definite historical periods fixed between major political events. There is no such thing as 'universal liberalism' in the sense that the ideology possesses a definable and unchanging essence everywhere and at every level of its expression, but the argument against stipulative definition holds just as good against a number of such definitions as against one. To define liberalism in England as essentially anti-state, and liberalism in Germany, between 1812 and 1918, as essentially nationalistic is no less a mistake than to define all genuine liberalism as Lockean. A tradition of discourse does not possess the coherence that admits of definition or definitions, and its life-span is determined by written and spoken contributions to it, not by political events. It is, in fact, extremely difficult to put dates to its life, before and after which it can definitely be said not to exist. A tradition of political thought is not the work of one mind, or identical minds, within a short period of time, and incoherence in its development does not introduce into it the kind of radical disjuncture which makes impossible the identification of the whole, so that we are obliged to talk about its quite separate national identities at different times. To be able to claim that there is more than one liberal tradition we have to be able to point to a protracted dispute between men claiming to be liberals, like that between revolutionary and democratic socialists during the present century over the principles of their doctrine, or show that one set of principles was substituted for another, which then became extinct, rather than being reapplied in changed circumstances. The truth is that once we try to define liberalism according to ideas of freedom, or any other concept plucked from the tradition of discourse in which it appears, we are likely to discover as many liberalisms as liberal writers. Certainly we would uncover more than Cranston has found. Smith, Shelley, Acton and Hobhouse could hardly, had they gathered, have failed to find much about which to disagree on the subject of freedom. But it would be ridiculous to say that the work of only one of them is typical of English liberalism.

It is true that, in the first instance, most liberal writers have addressed themselves to political issues of immediate concern to their fellow countrymen. It is obvious from the last chapter that Milton, Locke and Mill were particularly interested in influencing contemporary opinion and events in England. At the same time their work was presented in a form likely to be of interest to a much wider audience, and it did attract and persuade readers beyond England's shores both soon and long after the events which occasioned its publication. As Martin's book, *Liberty*, suggests, the most famous liberal theorists in America are Englishmen. In this and the following chapter we shall find that neither national boundaries nor time isolated the major liberal writers from one another. They are amongst the most widely educated men of their generations and probably the most keenly aware of their own intellectual heritage of all modern political thinkers. The facts are that Kant was a keen student of Locke, and Green of Kant. Mill did not consider the concerns of von Humboldt foreign to his own, and de Tocqueville read Mill with profit and approval. Spencer attracted a personal following in America, and, today, the Kantian interpretation of justice provided by the American John Rawls is as popular in England as that provided by the Belgian Chaim Perelman. The rise of national socialist and fascist parties in Europe was attacked by liberals whose native language is English no less virulently than by Karl Popper, Benedetto Croce and Ortega y Gasset whose native languages are German, Italian and Spanish respectively. Liberals have never seen the threats to the way of life of which they approve as being a purely national concern. Although there is no such thing as universal liberalism, in the sense that it has only one theme throughout, it is an internationalist and an international doctrine. Its prescriptions are addressed to the world and its major authors have international reputations.

To reveal something of the dimensions of the liberal theory of government, and to establish that these transcend the spatio-temporal divisions of political culture, it is proposed to present their development over four centuries in a variety of countries. The presentation, is, for the sake of the structure of this book, divided into two parts, the first covering the seventeenth and eighteenth centuries, and the second covering the nineteenth and twentieth centuries. It spans a wide spectrum of political opinion. Even so, although the work of writers placed at the ends of the spectrum may appear disparate, each and every contributor will be found to share important political ideas with his neighbours, and through them with others who have been known as liberals—a fact of which they are aware. Similarity is not itself the principle by which their work has been selected. The criterion of simi-larity leads to the error of essentialism. Whether or not the work of any particular writer has been included in or excluded from the survey is determined by his having, or not having, the historical reputation of being a liberal, or ancestor of liberal thinking. Amongst those excluded are Buchanan, Althusius and Mariana. Their works appear to be as capable of inspiring a liberal as those of Milton, Grotius and Locke, but they did not command the deference of the eighteenth- and nineteenth-century advocates of the doctrine. To include every writer who has said something that looks like what we may choose to call liberalism will inevitably admit a large number of writers whose contribution to political thought happens to be to other teachings.

We are here concerned with the meaning of liberalism for liberals. What it has meant to men of other persuasions is not unimportant, but this tells us about their own political beliefs, not the beliefs of those whom we are here concerned to understand. In the Marxist account of liberalism, for example, the whole tradition is presented as a manifestation of the interest of the bourgeois class. It has no independent life of its own. Liberalism is assimilated within the structure of Marxist analysis. Crawford Macpherson's treatment of Hobbes, Harrington and Locke in his book, *The Political Theory of Possessive Individualism*, illustrates the point perfectly. Harrington is portrayed as trying to give the Marxist idea of the liberal theory of politics, and of doing it badly. Macpherson tells us that 'we may say of Harrington that the theoretical strength of his system lay in his recognition and acceptance of possessive market relations and motivation, and its theoretical weakness in his failure to see fully or state clearly all the assumptions that were involved'.[4] The possibility that Harrington was not a Marxist's idea of a liberal at all cannot arise. For the Marxist, political theories, other than Marxism, are all manifestations of the concrete socio-economic relationships of their time, and Harrington's cannot be an exception. His has to be the subjective bourgeois consciousness portrayed by Marx as peculiar to the epoch. A little further on Macpherson tells us that changes in nineteenth-century economic and social relationships, intelligible only in the context of Marxism, reveal the extent to which the kind of liberalism represented by Harrington is archaic. Liberalism, in this view, never had a chance of standing on its own feet and the fact is not surprising.

Ideologies are concerned to change and not to understand the world in any academic sense. They cannot, therefore, be expected to admit the kind of incongruousness that destroys their power to provoke the desired response. To place Harrington on the same footing as Marx in a Marxist interpretation of political life can only destroy the meaning of Marxism. We cannot be a liberal and a Marxist at one and the same time. To mix liberal and Marxist beliefs can only confuse us ideologically, and the confused are incapable of effective communication. To give an objective account of any ideology it is necessary to give it from a non-ideological point of view, and this Macpherson has failed to do. He has totally failed to map the geography of liberal ideas, as distinct from taking us on a guided tour through the landscape of Marxist thought.

In the following presentation of the spectrum of liberal thought the ideas of men who have not only inspired liberals, but have been admired by adherents of other ideologies, make an appearance. They are to be taken as marking the limits of liberal thought. William Godwin and Sir Henry Maine, for example, are men with more than one reputation. The former has been praised by anarchists and the latter by conservatives. There are also a number of political thinkers who, like Samuel Taylor Coleridge and Sir James Mackintosh, abandoned their early enthusiasm for liberalism and accepted a more conservative teaching. There are others like Johann Fichte and Harold Laski who abandoned liberalism for the more radical politics of nationalism and socialism respectively. Their work may also be taken as marking the limits of the liberal tradition. It is as futile as it is unnecessary to attempt to determine *a priori* the limits of the liberal position by some calculations as to the maximum allowable distance a writer may stand to left or right of the essential centre of the doctrine before being barred from inclusion in its territory. Traditions of ideological writings do not have definable centres any more than they have fixed circumferences. The simple fact that a writer is recognized by liberals as having influenced the development of liberalism is all that is required to qualify him for admission to these pages.

Needless to say, it is not intended that the following two chapters present a detailed picture of liberalism any more than it can produce a perfectly harmonious one. It is a picture of liberalism viewed from a distance—a panoramic vision—which is intended to reveal something of the unity and interrelationships, without obliterating the variety and range, of its subject-matter. The central concern of this chapter, then, is neither the symbolic form of liberalism nor the arguments which make up the liberal tradition of discourse, although something of both inevitably makes an appearance. It is to the liberal position on the organization of good government and the purpose of desirable political action that our attention is now directed.

The Right to Resist Tyranny

One of the first and most celebrated presentations of the case against absolute government favoured by liberals is to be found in the Huguenot tract *Vindiciae Contra Tyranos* first published in France in 1581 and in England in 1622. Here it is asserted that no man has a right to the unlimited exercise of sovereign power, since whatever the extent of his power, no man has the authority to direct others contrary to the revealed will of God. The existence of political society may not be seen as independent of God's church. It is a prerequisite for the protection of the faithful and involves the performance of Christian duties. The ruler has the duty of protecting the subject and enforcing justice, and the subject has the duty of rendering such service as is required by his ruler in order that he fulfil his obligations to God. Subject and ruler are to be understood as bound by a covenant, and in the event of either party violating its provisions all have the duty to punish the wrong-doer. If a ruler abuses the power of his office, he, no less than the subject who breaks the law, is justly punished. Every violation of law made in accordance with scripture constitutes an attack on true religion. It follows that not only is it lawful to resist a tyrant, but that all who do not 'ought to know that in neglecting to perform this duty they make themselves culpable of the same crime, and shall bear the like punishment with their king'.[5] In the *Vindiciae* we have the explicit statement that a king is no more than God's representative on earth responsible to God for the enforcement of His Law in the eyes of

His people. It has always to be remembered that kingship is not lordship. The 'name of a king signifies not an inheritance, nor a property, nor a usufruct, but a charge, office and procuration'.[6]

The central teaching of the *Vindiciae* is to be found in the two greatest treatises on law written by Protestant jurists in the sixteenth century: Hugo Grotius' *De Juri Belli ac Libri Tres*, published in Holland in 1625, and Samuel Pufendorf's *Du Juri Natural et Gentium*, published in Sweden in 1672. Both authors conceive civil society as originating in man's appreciation of the benefits to be enjoyed under a government dedicated to the impartial administration of justice. It consists in 'a complete association of freemen, joined together for the enjoyment of rights and their common interest'.[7] It originates in a pact to which 'it is necessary for each and all to give their consent'. Thereafter the form of government to be established is to be determined 'by the agreement of the majority . . .' And, finally, through a further pact 'the rulers bind themselves to the core of the common security and safety, and the rest to render them obediences . . .'[8] It follows that a ruler who invaded the rights of his subjects is justly resisted. There can be no form of personal loyalty to a monarch which can override each and every man's obligation to follow the dictates of his own conscience. In matters concerning the government of man the only will that may properly prevail is the will of God.

That a civil society is a voluntary association and government a public trust in the eyes of God is also the insistence of Milton in his *The Tenure of Kings and Magistrates*, published in 1648. We are informed that a ruler who abuses his power must be brought to trial by the magistrates. Failing this it is legitimate for 'any, who have the power, to call to account a tyrant, or wicked King, and after due conviction, depose and put him to death . . .'[9] The authority of government cannot be exercised in the manner of a private right. It may only be exercised 'in execution of those laws which they the people had themselves made or assented to'.[10] Milton wrote *The Tenure of Kings and Magistrates* specifically to justify the trial and execution of Charles I. The argument is brief and to the point. Later in the century Sidney and Locke took the opportunity to elaborate the case for responsible government when replying to the arguments they found in Filmer's *Patriarcha: A Defence of the Natural Power of Kings against the Unnatural Liberty of the People.* This defence of rule by divine right was printed in 1680, some forty years after it was written. It was published to assist the cause of Charles II in the Exclusion Crisis of 1679–80 and became a classic Tory text during the reign of James II. Sidney's reply, *Discourses Concerning Government*, was written between 1680 and 1683, but it was not published until 1698. Sidney was executed for alleged complicity in the Rye House Plot and his work declared treasonable in 1683. Locke's *Two Treatises of Government* was conceived prior to 1688, but not published until the following year. It is fair to say that the publication of the work of Sidney and Locke on government owes much to the success of the Glorious Revolution.

Filmer's argument is straightforward. It is that society is one extended family and all authority exercised within it is paternal. In the case of political authority it consists of the hereditary right of kings to exercise the authority God gave to Adam over his children—an authority which the eldest male member of the family has inherited in every generation by right of primogeniture. Filmer emphatically rejects any suggestion that a monarch is responsible to anyone other than God and that his people have any right to judge his conduct.

As far as Sidney and Locke were concerned Filmer's justification of passive obedience amounted to nothing less than the advocation of slavery. Locke's opening sentence of the first of his *Two Treatises* expressed their common indignation:

> Slavery is so vile and miserable an estate of man, and so directly opposite to the generous temper and courage of our nation, that it is hardly to be conceived that an Englishman, much less a gentleman, should plead for it.[11]

Both perceived that Filmer's objectionable conclusions followed from his account of the origin of political society, and both presented an alternative account. According to Sidney, Filmer is quite mistaken in believing that political society is simply an extension of Adam's family. He suggests that Adam's descendants were originally quite independent of one another:

> We have already seen . . . that every man continued in this liberty, till the number so increased, that they became troublesome and dangerous to each other; and finding no other remedy to the disorder growing, or like to grow among them, joined families into one civil body, that they might the better provide for the conveniency, safety and defence of themselves and their children.[12]

Locke argues that Adam had no paternal authority over his adult children, or they over their own issues once they came of age. Even supposing that they had, it is now impossible to determine who has inherited this authority in the present generation since there exists no recognized rule of succession, or evidence of its having been consistently applied. We can only conclude that political society originated in a compact whereby men in a state of nature surrendered to each other their right to punish any who violated the law of nature. This right was then placed in the hands of those commissioned to form a government so long as it is exercised only to enforce the rule of just laws. It is strictly a limited right:

> And whosoever in authority exceeds the power given him by law, and makes use of the force he has under his command, to compass that upon the subject, which the law allows not, ceases . . . to be a magistrate, and . . . may be opposed as any other man, who by force invades the right of another.[13]

Sidney reached the same conclusion. Political authority is vested in the office of a ruler:

> No man has it for himself, or from himself: but for and from those (who) before he had it were his equals, that he may do good to them.[14]

A ruler who invades the rights and harms the interests of his subjects is wholly responsible for the revolt which actions of this kind occasion. It cannot be denied that 'the peace may be broken upon just grounds, and it may be neither a crime nor infamy to do it'.[15]

No doubt it was the fate of James II rather than the cogency of the arguments of Sidney and Locke, which destroyed absolutism in England. But, in the eighteenth century, to both English and Continental authors, what had been a mere theory appeared to have been made an established practice. Voltaire's opinion is typical:

> The English are the only people upon earth who have been able to prescribe limits to the power of kings resisting them, and who, by a series of struggles, have at length established that wise and happy form of government where the prince is all-powerful to do good, and at the same time is restricted from committing evil; where the nobles are great without insolence or lordly power, and the people share in the government without confusion.[16]

From fear of persecution the *Vindiciae* was published anonymously. For holding political opinions similar to those expressed in it Locke suffered exile and Sidney execution. But by 1788 Joseph Priestley no longer considered it necessary even to attack the doctrine to which his heroes had been opposed. In his lectures, *History and General Policy*, he proclaimed:

> The notion that kings reign by divine right, independently of the designation of the people, and therefore that they are not accountable to them for the exercise of their power, is now universally and deservedly exploded.[17]

The events of 1688 were, as Jean-Louis de Lolme observed, decisive as far as the cause of royal absolution in England was concerned:

> The principles of passive obedience, the Divine and indefeasible right of kings, in a word, the whole scaffolding of fatal, because false, notions, by which the royal authority had till then been supported, fell to the ground: and in the

room of it were substituted the more solid and desirable
foundations of the love of order, and a sense of the necessity
of civil government among mankind.[18]

What form did these foundations take, and who designed
them?

The Way to Maintain Liberty

On the first page of *The Spirit of the Laws*, published in 1748,
Montesquieu, one of the architects of the new doctrine, states the
principle essential to the understanding of his work:

> Since we observe that the world, though formed by the
> motion of matter, and void of understanding, subsists
> through so long a succession of ages, its motions must
> certainly be directed by invariable laws; and could we
> imagine another world, it must also have constant rules, or
> it would inevitably perish.[19]

Montesquieu proceeds to argue that there are similar laws
guaranteeing the stability of society. Their operation is an
observable fact. Whether or not a law is good or bad is a normative judgment, but whether or not it will work is not. The
effectiveness of legal systems is the subject of political science.
The business of law is the creation of liberty, and by liberty we
are to understand that 'right of doing whatever the law permits,
and if a citizen could do what they forbid he would no longer be
possessed of liberty, because all his fellow-citizens would have the
same power'.[20] But to preserve liberty governments not only
have to make and enforce law: they have to abide by it, and this
duty they are most likely to fulfil where their constitution provides for the separation of their executive, legislative and judicial
functions. The careful classification and comparison of political
experiences clearly indicate that the effect of this separation is to
avoid both the accumulation of power, which may readily be
abused, and the chaos involved in the re-establishing of equilibrium by revolution, when the abuse has occurred. Political

instability is usually occasioned by the abuse of power and the abuse of power is facilitated by the absence of checks and balances.

Priestley harboured the same preoccupations with liberty and stability, balance, and harmony. He is of the opinion that:

> When a state cannot be preserved by the universal, or very general desire of the people, it may be saved by the balancing of those powers which would tend to destroy it; and as all different orders of men naturally wish for more power, and every individual wishes to rise above his neighbour, all governments, may in fact, be considered as in this state. It is therefore of importance so to arrange the different parts of the constitution as that a struggle for power may be prevented from having any dangerous effect. And perhaps it may be asserted that the more distinct interests there are in a state, the easier it will be to preserve the balance of power within it.[21]

The two principal threats to liberty and stability perceived by Priestley are tyrannical monarchy and a majority of citizens intent on seizing and exercising power in their own interest. Properly conceived government represents the interest of all and is responsible to all. The members of government must be independent of all sectarian views: 'No maxims or rules of policy can be binding upon them, but such as they themselves shall judge to be conducive to the public good.'[22] The same point of view expressed by Montesquieu in France, and Priestley in England, is to be found in *The Federalist Papers*, published in America in 1788. James Madison emphatically pronounced that the 'accumulation of all power, legislative, executive and judiciary, in the hands, whether of one, or few, or many and whether hereditary, self-appointed, or elective, may justly be pronounced the very definition of tyranny'.[23] In the proposed Federal Republic of the United States of America every possible precaution must be taken to balance sectional interests:

> Whilst all authority ... will be derived from and dependent on the society, the society itself will be broken into so many

parts, interests and classes of citizens, that the rights of individuals, or of the minority, will be in little danger from interested combinations of the majority . . .[24]

Madison's views are similar to those of his contemporaries, Thomas Jefferson and Alexander Hamilton. The stress that all three give to the right to private property is related to their rejection of a centralized system of government favoured by the enlightened despots of Europe. The spirit of federalism is decentralization. The founding fathers of America firmly believed in the desirability of as many men as possible owning property and being consulted on political matters which concerned them. They rejected absolutely the possibility that America be governed by the unrestrained majority at any particular moment, and the possibility that she should continue to be ruled by hereditary power of the kind from which she had recently declared her independence.

In the political thought of Montesquieu, de Lolme, Priestley and Madison we can detect an emphasis, absent in the work of Milton, Sidney and Locke. The preoccupation with balance is more explicit, not only in terms of a constitutional separation of the functions of government, but also in terms of avoiding the domination of public affairs by any one section of society. For Milton, Sidney and Locke the threat to civil liberty came from a monarch claiming a divine and hereditary right to absolute power. For Montesquieu, de Lolme, Priestley and Madison the danger of a narrow-minded majority gaining a monopoly of political power was an equal and, for the last two authors, a more immediate threat.

Two other changes in the work of the eighteenth-century ancestors of liberalism are of importance to the development of the Newtonian framework of their point of view: one, a diminution of the importance of revelation as a source of knowledge of the proper constitution of the body politic, and two, a decline in the significance of the original Christian doctrine of natural law employed by Hooker and Locke to indicate the limits of legitimate political action. As we have seen, Montesquieu, de Lolme,

Priestley and Madison substituted, for a predominantly theological argument, something more like a science of politics. They do not rely upon the biblical account of man's past to explain the origin and determine the form of legitimate government. They prefer to argue that the study of ancient and modern experience suggests that one form of government is conducive to stability, security and prosperity, and that this must be considered the form most compatible with God's plan for the creation. This thesis, a major tenet of liberalism in the second half of the eighteenth century, is developed at length in the work of Adam Smith, making him one of the universally revered figures in the history of the tradition. His two most influential publications are *The Theory of Moral Sentiments*, which first appeared in 1759, and *An Enquiry into the Nature and Causes of the Wealth of Nations*, first published in 1776.

More clearly than any other writer Smith spelt out the new liberal position. Man's political, social and economic orders are to be seen as the natural consequence of his desire for universal security, sympathy with his fellows and concern for his own material well-being. The spontaneous interaction of men has, with the guidance of reason, led to the formation of a pattern of behaviour conducive to the preservation of their species. The resolving of public and private disagreement according to legal procedures, the application of impartial judgment to moral questions, and the cultivation of prudence and enterprise in economic activity have paved the way to peace and prosperity. The existence of the human order can only be seen as confirming the Christian opinion that the 'happiness of mankind, as of all other rational creatures, seems to have been the original purpose intended by the Author of Nature when he brought them into existence'.[25] The permanence of human society makes it foolish to doubt that 'by acting according to the dictates of our moral faculties we necessarily pursue the most effective means of promoting the happiness of mankind and may therefore be said, in some sense, to co-operate with the Deity, and to advance, so far as is in our power, the plan of providence'.[26] However, Smith warns his readers that it would be imprudent to ignore the fact that there exist arrogant and foolish men who 'imagine that to be the wisdom of man, which in reality is the wisdom of God'.[27] Men such as these are all too ready to attempt the reorganization of society according to some preconceived plan. They are particularly dangerous in politics:

> The man of system . . . is so often enamoured with the supposed beauty of his own ideal plan of government, that he cannot suffer the smallest deviation from any part of it . . . he seems to imagine that he can arrange the different members of a great society with as much ease as the hand arranges the different pieces upon the chess-board . . . but . . . on the great chess-board of human society, every single piece has a principle of its own, altogether different from that which the legislature might choose to impress upon it. If these two principles coincide and act in the same direction, the game of human society will go on easily and harmoniously, and is very likely to be happy and successful. If they are opposite or different, the game will go on miserably, and the society must be at all times in the highest degree of disorder'.[28]

Smith is firmly of the opinion that a wise government will avoid interference in the natural order of society. It will confine its attention to reinforcing the rules of justice, without the recognition of which 'the immense fabric of human society . . . must in a moment crumble into atoms'.[29] One of the implications of his conclusion is that governments should never forget that the 'peace and order of society is more important than even the relief of the miserable'.[30] For Smith, the title of every man to the fruits of his own labour is his most fundamental right. Where it is infringed by a government liberty is radically diminished. For example, to 'hinder . . . the farmer from sending his goods at all times to the best market, is evidently to sacrifice the ordinary laws of justice to an idea of public utility, to a sort of reasons of state: an act of legislative authority which ought to be exercised only, which can be pardoned only, in cases of the most urgent necessity'.[31] The distinction Smith made between civil society, based on the concepts of liberty and justice, and the state, governed by the utilitarian considerations of wealth, welfare and security is an important step in liberal thinking. It points the way firstly to the difference between the citizen's obligation to comply with the decisions of legal government, and the desire of the subject to resist the power of the servants of the state; and secondly, between the defence of the liberty of the individual through a legislature responsible to the people, and the promotion of the interests of the state as its professional servants conceive it.

If any one liberal writer deserves the title of Newton of the social sciences it is surely Smith. In his work, the transfer of the basis of the orthodox understanding of politics and economics from revelation to observation is virtually complete. His account of human relationships and human nature is primarily sociological and psychological rather than theological and metaphysical. In this respect it may be classed with the work of Bentham and Spencer.

A clinical account of the development of liberalism would, at this point, proceed to an examination of eighteenth-century German and nineteenth-century English and French writers. It would ignore the confusion of the English ideological confrontations of the late eighteenth century. However, to ignore the contribution to liberalism of late eighteenth-century English thinkers would detract from the historical accuracy of our picture of universal liberalism. In the work of Paine, Godwin and Bentham there are to be found strands of thought which made a contribution to liberalism, in spite of the fact that they do not directly tie in with those supplied by Priestley and Smith. Indeed they are closely related to lines of thought emphatically rejected by liberals writing at a later date. As such, they may be taken to mark the boundaries of the liberal inheritance as it stood at the end of the eighteenth century.

The Organization of Government

At the height of their fame Paine, Godwin and Bentham were, in their individual ways, radical democrats. They pressed the attack on personal and autocratic rule to the point where no government, or only government directly representing the interests of the people, is acceptable. Paine and Bentham completely abandoned the view that government should be independent of the influence of every section of the community. They came to the conclusion that political power is delegated power. Its direction is, they proclaimed, the inalienable right of the people. For Paine this right is a natural right. For Bentham it is a right every government must confer on its subjects if it is to fulfil its moral obligation to promote the greatest happiness of men who are the best judge of their own interests. Both found little to admire in existing English political practice as defended by Blackstone and Burke. Both discarded the doctrine of a balance of power held by King, Lords and Commons. They believed that all the business of government is carried on by members of the one privileged section of the community. Paine considered the British government to be the same despotism which originated with a 'French bastard landing with an armed banditti, and established himself king of England against the consent of the natives . . .'[32] Bentham characterized it as a system of government in which 'aptitude, with relation to the exercise of political power, is inversely as the aptitude of man's place in the composite scale of political influence'.[33] Godwin, the most radical of the three, held in 1793, when his major work *Enquiry Concerning Political Justice* was published, that the exercise of political power is largely unnecessary and likely to become altogether undesirable. He confidently looked forward to a future in which men would choose to live in small self-governing, self-sufficient communities, without private property. Here, to the common welfare, each would contribute according to his ability and, for himself, take according to his need.

Paine, Bentham and Godwin arrived independently at the same conclusion, namely, that the purpose of government is the promotion of happiness. They are not in agreement as to how this purpose can be achieved, but each is, in his own way, a committed individualist. Paine located the autonomy of the individual in the possession of natural rights, Bentham in self-interest and

Godwin in private conscience. Each contributed to the liberal tradition in spite of the fact that the arguments they advanced in favour of direct democracy were to be repudiated. Their rejection of aristocratic privilege was acceptable, but their faith in the rationality of the common man was not. The course of the French Revolution and the emergence of a politically conscious industrial proletariat suggested to the orthodox middle-class liberal that the theorists admired by the radical wing of the movement had, in rejecting one form of tyranny, made way for another.

Paine's attack on Burke in *The Rights of Man*, Bentham's attack on Blackstone in *A Fragment on Government*, and Godwin's attack on Malthus in *Of Population* had the effect of distinguishing liberalism from the progressively more conservative disposition of the orthodox Whigs. In arguing for the end of political patronage, the extension of the franchise and in favour of penal and legal reform, the radicals bequeathed a political programme of increasing prominence in nineteenth-century liberal politics. But it cannot be claimed that this programme was peculiar to liberalism and, as suggested, the theoretical justifications advanced by the radical liberals in support of it were not adopted by the major liberal theorists of the nineteenth century. Along with the case for popular government, Godwin's faith in natural justice, Paine's belief in the rights of men and Bentham's commitment to egotistical hedonism found few uncritical admirers amongst later liberal authors. Godwin eventually came to be seen as a precursor of anarchism, Paine of chartism and Bentham of Fabianism. The two eighteenth-century writers who elaborated the metaphysical foundations of the enduring liberal concepts of liberty and justice are Fichte, in the first phase of his development, and Kant. The acceptable utilitarian justification of political action was to be furnished by Mill. The one English eighteenth-century work which enjoyed undiminished influence on the nineteenth-century evolution of liberalism was Smith's *The Wealth of Nations*. If the number of times it was reprinted and quoted is any indication of its authority it has no rival. Both Paine and Godwin died forgotten men.

Fichte and Kant set out to elaborate a more coherent account of the nature of liberty and justice than they found in the work of Grotius, Pufendorf and Locke. Fichte, who published *The Science of Rights* in 1796, perceived that man is able to live in association with his fellows with a minimum of conflict by virtue of the fact that he can make and follow rules. In this man is distinct from other members of the animal kingdom, for which reason justice, rights, duties, and liberty are peculiar to his society. Outside human society they do not exist. Fichte's principal objective is to demonstrate that rational man 'attains rights only in a community with others as indeed he only becomes man . . . through intercourse with others'.[34] The notion that, as an individual, man was temporarily or logically prior to society was thereby effectively challenged. It was never again to play the part it had previously played in the liberal tradition. Fichte affirmed that justice is pure rationality in social relationships. Reason and law together create the possibility of liberty and justice amongst men. The one points to what the other requires in human relationships; namely, respect for other persons.

Kant, who published *The Metaphysical Elements of Justice* in 1797, argues that because man is a rational creature he can distinguish between right and wrong actions. Indeed, man cannot be considered an independent being unless it is evident that he has this capacity. It follows that if a man is to demonstrate his independence he must be allowed the freedom necessary to exercise his moral judgment. Since the moral character of an action consists in its being performed for the right kind of reason, the independence of men cannot be promoted by forcing them to discharge their duties to others. Morality is inseparable from liberty. Without the spontaneous participation of free men, force, not reason, forms the basis of social relationships, and force invariably destroys the moral character of those who exercise it no less than it inhibits the development of moral character in those who are subject to it. Justice, according to Kant, requires the recognition of moral obligation and morality requires that we 'treat humanity, whether in your own person or in that of another, always as an end and never as a means only'.[35] Every moral man is obliged to act in the way in which he would approve every other man acting were he in the same situation. Justice prevails in society when 'the freedom of your will is compatible with the freedom of everyone according to a universal law'.[36]

The political implications of this analysis are straightforward for its originators. There are no reasonable grounds upon which a government may claim the right to make and enforce laws with a view to obliging men to be good. Laws can only create the circumstances in which men may, by freely choosing to act justly, develop their own moral character. Where men break the law and violate the freedom of others they may be justly punished. Punishment is to be understood as a retributive act, not as a deterrent threat or a reforming influence.

Kant, and Fichte during his liberal years, took the view that the business of government is the making and application of rules in accordance with the principles of justice. It is not the pursuit of a policy designed to improve the people. Its role is to arbitrate rather than dictate, and it is more important that it be impartial than representative. Both favoured the republican form of government, but they insisted that the exercise of its power must be strictly constitutional. The prospect of popular government they found no less a threat to liberty and justice than the despotism of one man. They also rejected the argument that, in desperate circumstances, violent revolution is justified. They looked to constitutional procedures to ensure the accountability of those elected to public office. The people themselves could not be relied upon to act justly once they took the law into their own hands. In Kant's view it is altogether more desirable that 'the will of the legislator . . . is irreproachable; the executive capacity of the chief magistrate is irresistible; and the adjudication of the supreme judge is unalterable'.[37] Each should, however, enjoy an authority absolute only in its appropriate field of exercise. Each should be subject to the authority of the other two within their spheres of jurisdiction. Beyond the official exercise of their authority every public servant and politician ought to respect the same laws and judicial processes as the ordinary citizen.

In order that the people be informed of any abuse of the authority vested in public offices Fichte proposed the installation of a body he called the *Ephorate*. Its members were to scrutinize the management of public affairs and call for passive resistance to illegitimate measures. Both he and Kant considered that political authority originates in the willing compliance of the citizen with decisions recognized to be just. Therefore, the perpetration of injustices must lead to the dissolution of the authority, or expulsion from office, of those responsible. This has itself to be conducted according to law. In every respect the survival of a civil society depends upon the application of rules.

In the mature work of Kant and the early work of Fichte we find the most elaborate and coherent presentation of the political theory of liberalism before its adherents were confronted with the problems of the nation state and industrial society. However, for all its sophistication, it embodies the same plea for constitutional rule and civil liberty made by the author of *Vindiciae*, and by Grotius, Pufendorf, Milton, Sidney and Locke, on religious grounds, and by Montesquieu, Priestley, Madison and Smith on the findings of their science of politics. It also embodies the same concern with justice and morality. The politics of liberalism are the politics of principle. Machiavelli's suggestion that a ruler should combine the cunning of a fox with the strength of a lion, Hobbes's conviction that covenants without the backing of the sword are but words and Hume's suggestion that men ought not to be encouraged to question long-established political beliefs are all firmly rejected in favour of perfect honesty, total obligation and fearless criticism of all human practices and received opinions.

Every writer whose work has received attention in the preceding pages has been included in the genealogy of liberalism by members of its family because he affirms that every man is responsible for his own conduct. This conduct is to be judged according to objective standards of moral value. The final authority in all human affairs is the conscience or reason of the private individual. This logically precludes the claims that it is legitimate for any man arbitrarily to impose his will on another. The sole foundation of public authority is the consent of those over whom it is exercised according to established rules and known standards. Quite explicitly they all agree that civil society originates and consists in the willing submission of every section of the community to the formation and administration of just laws without regard to their social and economic inequalities.

The original formation of the liberal position on the constitution and function of government was a response to the challenge to individual liberty presented by the seventeenth-century claim to kingship on grounds of divine and hereditary right. The doctrine was eventually redeployed to meet what was seen to be the equally dangerous challenge to individual rights presented by the claim to absolute sovereignty made on behalf of the common man. For the most part the liberal theory of government is, throughout this period, a Protestant doctrine. With few exceptions the authors whose work has been examined in this chapter are of this faith. They approached politics from the position that no man can afford to surrender his responsibility to obey the dictates of divine reason under threat of an arbitrary and despotic power wielded by a mere mortal. The transference of the source of political knowledge from divine revelation to human observation, leading to the elaboration of a science of politics, did not alter the fundamental liberal conviction that every man is under an obligation to serve the highest purpose reason can reveal to him, and that this is the purpose the Creator intended him to serve. The values liberals hold dear are absolute not relative values. Parliamentary institutions and the legal framework of civil society are admitted to be artificial. They would not exist but for the courageous sacrifice of immediate private advantage by farsighted men. However, although they are only human constructs, in need of constant repair, for liberals the order they reflect transcends the arbitrary and transitory character of human experience which prevails outside the relationships established in accordance with it. Where recognized, the liberal order of justice is eternal, immutable and universal. Where men have refused to recognize its impartial jurisdiction their lives are capricious, precarious and chaotic. In the final analysis liberals believe that all human achievements presuppose public respect for law and order. There can be no freedom and no justice without it. The struggle for the institution of civil society and the creation of constitutional government is nothing less than the defence of civilization in the world. The liberal concept of citizenship is to be applied to men regardless of their pedigree. It is not an identity restricted to members of a religion, a nation, a class or a race. Calvin's *Institutes*, von Treischke's *Politics*, Marx's *Communist Manifesto* and Hitler's *Mein Kampf* are each addressed to an exclusive group. They are not intended to inspire Catholics, Frenchmen, capitalists and Jews, only Protestants, Germans, workers and Aryans respectively. In contrast, even the most Protestant of the liberal theorists was prepared to accept Catholic converts to his political beliefs. It is to mankind as a whole that liberals have, without major exception, addressed themselves. Their fellow countrymen have been the most immediate audience, but never an exclusive one. There are no national liberalisms.

4 The Dialectic of Liberal Doctrine

A chronological reading of liberal writers of the nineteenth and twentieth centuries might lead one to believe that their works constitute a continual revision of a classical inheritance. Mill and Spencer, Green and Hobhouse, John Dewey and Walter Lippman, for example, claimed to have set out to recast the form and change the content of a received doctrine they deemed to be misleading. Their works were intended as corrections to the misapplication of liberal principles and the false propositions about the political world made by their predecessors. However, it cannot be the case that they revised either the work of any particular liberal writer, or the tradition of liberal thinking to which they made a contribution. Liberal writers are mistaken in their belief that their principles, properly based and applied, are indispensable to the successful conduct of the practice of politics, and that their propositions as to the appearance of political reality are factually correct. Liberalism is not the principles of the practice of politics or the set of true descriptions of the world in which it is conducted. The liberal tradition is incapable of logical coherence and correspondence to a given reality. But because liberal authors have supported incompatible policies, or because they have emphasized the value of first this and then that feature of political experience, it does not follow that liberalism is a failure. It has neither to be a coherent argument nor an objective observation. It succeeds as an elaborate on-going evaluation of human circumstances within the changing context of which, changing significance is ascribed to selected relationships and events. There is no accumulating knowledge of the world to which an ideology relates. The ideologist writes about the world in which we live and this is neither a finished artefact nor is it unalterable like the past to which the historian refers, or the impersonal external world the scientist examines in his laboratory. It is a world all men continually change by action.

During the nineteenth century the picture of political relationships presented by liberal writers did bear a relationship to the political practice of Western European, English and American democrats. Their practice was one of which the liberal theorists could largely approve. There is, for example, a parallel to be drawn between Mill's *Considerations on Representative Government* and the Victorian House of Commons. The two are contingent. However, a contingent relationship is altogether different from both a logical and a causal one. The relationship between the political practice of liberals and liberal ideology is one of compatibility, not one of entailment or inevitability. The Victorian was neither logically compelled nor psychologically forced to think or act in the way prescribed by liberal theorists. There were some capable of articulating a liberal view of the world, who were also capable of acting in a way that liberals did approve. There were others who could do the former but not the latter; and yet others who did the latter but not the former, in the sense that they lived a life of the kind which liberals could approve, but subscribed to another ideology—Frederick Engels is an example.

Liberal writers, to a large extent, provided for the majority the conceptual framework of Victorian politics and American capitalism at the turn of the century, but this fact could not compel the adherents of other ideologies to abandon their own vision of experience. Late nineteenth-century American and Western European society was not a liberal society. It was a society that could be seen from a liberal point of view. It could also be seen, equally clearly, from a socialist and conservative one. The fact that liberals largely approved of a particular society, as they conceived it, does not make it a liberal society. Presumably, if it were a liberal society it would be impossible to see it from a socialist or conservative point of view. The facts would refuse to fit these theories. The theories could not accommodate them. It is

The Dialectic of Liberal Doctrine

not the case that liberals did not *see* the relationships which were seen as evils by socialists and conservatives. They simply did not see them *as* evils. Ideologists invariably see what they believe. They do not believe what they see. What they make is an evaluation, not an observation. Were they ever to have an objective view of the world their theory would indeed be the mirror of contemporary practice. Every one of them, who is not in error, would then have exactly the same vision of experience, and it would be impossible to refute the claim that it is their theory that we see in practice.

However, no ideology, liberalism included, is, or can be, an accurate description of political experience. All ideologists seek to change the world into something it would not otherwise be. The ideology that merely reflects the world as it is could prescribe no more than that we accept it as a description.

Each and every ideology is an independent way in which experience may be interpreted. The significance any one ideology ascribes to a political phenomenon is peculiar to itself. An ideology is not an hypothesis that may be verified in a laboratory, where the principles of the practice of conducting experiments neither determines the results nor their implications for science as a whole. In contrast, the political practice of the ideologically committed, no matter what its outcome, may be taken to confirm the interpretation of events the principles of that ideology prescribe. For example, the fact that the proletarian revolution has not materialized in Britain is not a refutation of Marxism. It is merely another fact of significance within the Marxist interpretation of history. It might, for example, be used to point to a relationship between capitalism and imperialism, as in *Imperialism: the Highest State of Capitalism*, by Lenin. Similarly, it is not possible to challenge the Marxist view of history by pointing to this or that event as an exception to the findings of that interpretation of the past. In the Marxist interpretation there can be no exceptions. Every past event is a manifestation of the dialectic of history. Moreover, no matter how many distinct past events it is claimed are explicable in terms of the Marxist interpretation nothing is thereby added to suggest that the theory is more

83

comprehensive than it might otherwise be thought to be. Every such example may serve only as an illustration of the Marxist thesis, and no amount of examples may serve any better than one. Any sense in which they significantly differ from one another is excluded by the Marxist interpretation. In short, by definition, as far as Marxists are concerned, all history is the history of class struggle. Something similar is true of liberalism. All events which helped to constitute the civil society liberals admire are necessarily progressive and all those which mark resistance to these changes are necessarily reactionary. By definition a civil society is more civilized than a feudal one. In the vocabulary of liberalism part of the meaning of the word civil is something open and progressive, and part of the meaning of the word feudal is something closed and reactionary. Moreover, it is this part of the meaning of these words that liberals have given us. For example, before Karl Popper published *The Open Society and its Enemies*, the whole sense in which we now understand a society to be open or closed was by no means clear. A society is not a shop or the frontiers of a state.

We may take it then that because an ideology is not an objective understanding of experience in the academic sense it is nonsense to speak of Mill having revised, at a later date, his opinions on state assistance to the poor expressed in the earlier additions of his *Principles of Political Economy*. He changed old for new opinion. Similarly it is nonsense to suggest that T. H. Green *revised* the liberal position on freedom of contract. There was no mistake to be corrected. Rather than revise his original contributions to liberalism Mill made another one in the same way that Green later made a fresh application of liberal principles to the changed conditions of industrial Britain. The result, in both cases, was a new contribution to liberal thinking. It was not the discovery of an improved, let alone the true, form of political thinking. While Green advocated the increase of state intervention, to secure what *he* understood to be the freedom of the individual, Spencer was advocating less intervention to secure what *he* took to be personal liberty. There is nothing fixed about the boundaries of an ideological vision of experience. Its boundaries are continually redrawn by those who are recognized to be its exponents. An ideology is all that it has been said to be by those who have commanded the adherence of others who claim to be of the same conviction. It is not possible that one variety of an ideology be shown to be genuine and the others false, because what constitutes the truth of an ideology is precisely what is in dispute. An ideological argument about orthodoxy has no independent referent outside of such disputes. It is without a standard to which an appeal can be made in the way that we may appeal to the logic of scientific understanding to determine whether or not a particular statement is or is not scientific. The disputes within a tradition of ideological argument are all part of that tradition. Indeed, it could not continue to exist without them.

An ideological work may be said to offer a picture of the world of human affairs. More specifically it may be said to sketch the geography of human relationships with a view to informing the reader, who can identify himself with the kind of person to whom the work is addressed, that it is reasonable that he should conduct himself in a particular way in relation to different kinds of person. The manner in which he should conduct himself is related to his seeing himself as a particular kind of person—the person idealized in the ideological picture as an individual—a proletarian or a German, for example. The explicit elaboration of the potential adherent's identity is crucial to the success of a piece of ideological writing. In the case of Marx's work, one of the critical stages in the argument is the affirmation that society has undergone a series of transformations culminating in the emergence of capitalist enterprise, and a legal system facilitating capital formation, at the expense of the working man. In consequence the working man, who conceives himself as a peasant bound by the obligations of a rural community and hierarchy, or as an individual bound by the obligations of contract peculiar to commercial society, is a victim of false consciousness. He is not living in the real world. The account of the past given by Marx serves to emphasize aspects of the working man's experience which encourage him to accept the designation proletarian, and not that of peasant or emerging entrepreneur. For those who

85

reject this identity Marxism offers no orientation when it comes to evaluating situations and alternative courses of action.

This, however, is not to readmit, by the back door, the thesis that it is the theory of Marxism that is put into practice. A theory that concludes that this or that is the case—for example, that working men are exploited—is incommensurable with a decision that this or that will be done. As a body of literature Marxism, like liberalism, can serve no other political purpose than to draw attention to what is, from one point of view, significant in experience, and to teach men a vocabulary with which they can communicate with others persuaded to take the same course of action that they wish to take. In locating what he believed to be wrong in the world, and indicating what might be done about it, Marx did not guarantee the revolutionary act. Men of ability commit revolutionary, as distinct from criminal, acts when they are sufficiently frustrated by injustice in the world. But the brutal fact is that we can accept an account of the world's imperfections, and an assessment of its potential for improvement, and say and do nothing. An ideology does not itself possess motive power. Not only can it fail to convert those who subscribe to other teaching, it can fail to move the demoralized or restrain the self-interested. Germany's domestic policy during World War II may be justified by the racist doctrines of national socialism, but it is doubtful that many members of the German state carried out that policy simply because they were persuaded by that teaching. If the case of Eichmann is anything to go by the historian will find that there were many motives. This, however, is not to say that a claim to be an adherent of an ideology is disingenuous. It is merely to emphasize the difference between a portrayal of the world and being in the world. Those who have found Marxism a convincing portrayal of the world did not become alienated from reading Marx, and they did not experience class war reading him. They could not discover what Marx called alienation and class war in Marx's writing. They were only able through reading to locate and articulate their experience of frustrations and conflict in Marxist terms. In some cases their experience was proletarian, in others, like that of Marx, it was not. An ideology enables us to focus our attention on events, and provides a way of talking about experience. It neither provides experience nor gives the motive power and form to activity whereby we gain experience. It can relate to action only where men do feel strongly about an existing situation or practice, and know how to change it. It cannot itself generate the necessary resolve or skill. Our qualities and abilities are rooted in concrete experience. They are generated in the course of life. They are part of what it is to be in the world. They are not, any more than a given situation, part of a commentary on the world. They can be referred to or called upon in a book, but they cannot be fabricated by words.

Few ideologists have been engaged in politics and many politicians have been incapable of articulating an ideological characterization of their practice. Liberalism, as a library of ideological writing, is far from being the whole inspiration of the political movement represented by liberal political parties. Their political practice does not follow from the tenets of liberal ideology any more than that ideology is an abridgment of that practice, or a summary of the salient points of that practice (an abridged practice presumably is a shortened practice).[1] An ideological treatise stands apart from practice. It offers a set of rules, not experience of their application. It is a systematic presentation of the conceptual framework for an evaluation of experience, which, as an attitude to life, also finds expression in life in the form of political activity; life is another medium of experience. Not all that we want can be found in words. Without action the sexually frustrated can find no satisfaction in a copy of the *Kama Sutra*. There is much that cannot be said, only done. It is not surprising that liberal politicians have often acted in a way that the liberal ideologist has found unsatisfactory. Their activity cannot be identified with liberalism. It is not the political theory in practice. We may sympathize with the politician who is impatient with the criticisms of the ideologists of his own persuasion, since it is judgment in political affairs, not judgment in ideological thinking, that he is exercising, and of the former he does at least have some experience. When the liberal ideologist has declared that liberal politicians are no longer pursuing the goals prescribed by the true principles of politics there has occurred no divide between theory and practice, since they are altogether different things, and correspondence was impossible between them in the first place.

Ideological disputes take place between ideologists, not ideologists and politicians. Ideologists are engaged in framing a picture of experience in which this or that feature is peculiarly significant and provocative. Politicians are engaged in deciding on such action as reform and revolution. The work of the former is done in the study, that of the latter within political institutions and organizations. There is a contingent relationship between the two, but it is as well to remember that it is decisions not conclusions that change the world, and it is conclusions and not decisions which help us to understand it. The ideologist, in furnishing the vocabulary of politics, and in locating the significant features of the political terrain from one point of view, can assist the gifted politician of the same persuasion in identifying and assessing conflicts and in formulating and justifying settlements. He can also call upon those who have the moral sense and ability to take advantage of circumstances favourable to a particular course of action. It matters not how those circumstances arose. There is a connection between Marx and the successful Russian Revolution just as there is between the Glorious Revolution in England and the work of Locke. But in both cases it is one of contingency. The politician in changing the world can determine the relevance of what an ideologist has said just as easily as the ideologist can inform the politician. The Glorious Revolution could not refute the work of Sir Robert Filmer, but it went a long way towards making his understanding of the world an anachronism. Similarly, the Russian Revolution made Marx famous. It helped to make his reputation in the same way that the Glorious Revolution made that of Locke. But the fact that Lenin was a Marxist did not determine his actions, as distinct from influence his ideological views, any more than his actions proved Marx right. The French Revolution could not expose the errors of Rousseau. It did not follow them. And the emergence of industrial capitalism did not prove the doctrine of laissez-faire to be false, but it did occasion a reapplication of liberal principles whereby the liberal value of a welfare state is admitted, and the dangers of nationalism to liberal aspirations are recognized. In this chapter, it is the rejection of some positions without, and the making of new departures within, the liberal tradition that we will be examining.

Popular Government and the Rise of Nationalism

Throughout the nineteenth and twentieth centuries liberal theorists steadfastly adhered to a belief in the possibility of moral, material and intellectual progress. The belief had, in France, been inspired by the vision of the leaders of the Enlightenment who were persuaded that, once the era of superstition and corruption sustained by the power of priests and aristocrats had been brought to its inevitable close, liberty and equality would be possessed by all. At the same time some of them expressed a belief in the right of the people to be masters of their own political destiny. Their will, it was affirmed, is necessarily sovereign, and its free exercise ought in no way to be circumscribed. Abbé Sieyès spoke for this section of Enlightenment opinion in 1789 when he published *What is the Third Estate?* 'The nation,' he wrote, 'is prior to everything. It is the source of everything. Its will is always legal; indeed it is the law itself.' Sieyès considered this proposition to be a self-evident truth. Its universal recognition had been delayed only by the condition of ignorance in which the people had been kept by their unscrupulous rulers.

> During the long night of feudal barbarism, it was possible to destroy the true relations between men, to turn all concepts upside down, and to corrupt all justice: but, as day dawns, so gothic absurdities must fly and the remnants of ancient ferocity collapse and disappear. This is quite certain.[2]

Sieyès considered that there is a necessary connection between the abolition of political ignorance and the creation of a national assembly to give expression to the will of the French nation. However, this conclusion, obvious to Sieyès writing during the early days of the French Revolution, was far from acceptable to his countrymen looking back, after the defeat of Napoleon, on the events to which the Revolution had led. Whilst retaining a qualified belief in progress the French liberals, Madame de Staël, Benjamin Constant, François Guizot and Alexis de Tocqueville, rejected the claim that it entailed popular self-government. They endorsed the Enlightenment opinion that progress involved the abolition of both feudal society and royal despotism, but they rejected the conclusion that the assertion of the will of the people was progressive. Popular government, according to de Staël, was no less inclined to violate the rule of law than despotic rule, and it was altogether less stable. If anything it tended to encourage the unscrupulous lust for power 'in those who are at the top of the wheel, the eager desire to make it revolve in those who are beneath'.[3] The result had been the creation of the condition of chaos in which an opportunist like Napoleon could be received as a liberator. It was forever power, not a passion for progress, that fired the imagination of the revolutionary leaders. They, least of all, had proved prepared to use their position to exercise a moderating influence on the misguided enthusiasm of the masses. It served their purpose to exacerbate the crisis, using it as the pretext for a period of autocratic rule when 'the remedy for popular passions is to be found, not in despotism, but in the sovereignty of law'.[4]

Constant, de Staël's friend and ally, regarded the original aims of the Revolution to be 'equality of citizens in the eyes of the law, liberty of conscience, safety of persons, the responsible independence of the press'.[5] But these goals had been betrayed. The vicious doctrine of Rousseau, that the will of the people is sovereign, had been applied by the leaders thrown up by the Revolution with the most pernicious effect. Unlimited power in the hands of men who claim to represent the nation is no less despotic than that in the hands of a man who claims to represent no one but himself. 'Rousseau failed to recognize this truth, and his error has made the *Social Contract*, so often invoked in favour of liberty, the most terrible support of all kinds of despotism.'[6]

Madame de Staël and Constant passed their judgment on the ideas current during the Revolution in the second decade of the nineteenth century, Guizot and de Tocqueville in the fourth, but they concur. In his *Democracy and its Mission* Guizot set out to show that, properly conceived, political activity is concerned to determine the rights and duties of the members of a legal association. The basis of government has therefore to be reason and not will. 'If in social relations,' he wrote, 'only the wills of individuals stood in opposition to one another, the problem would not admit of solution.' [7] To claim that the will of the people is sovereign is to deny that the people have obligations, and this itself negates the very idea of a legal association. De Tocqueville agreed. A liberal society was founded upon the rule of law not the will of the people. De Tocqueville believed that, because the original aspirations of the French Revolution had been perverted by its radical leadership, the world must now look to America, not France, for its liberal inspiration. In his most famous work, *Democracy in America*, published in two parts in 1838 and 1840, he took the view that it is in the new world that there is now the best chance that a society will be formed in which 'all men would feel an equal love and respect for the laws of which they consider themselves the authors; in which the authority of the government would be respected as necessary, though not as divine; and in which the loyalty of the subject to the chief magistrate would not be a passion, but a quiet and national persuasion'. [8] What is more, he is of the opinion that unless the American example of democratic government is taken by his countrymen to be their model, 'if the peaceable domination of the majority be not founded amongst us in time, we shall sooner or later fall under the unlimited authority of a single man'. [9]

De Tocqueville found in America 'an extraordinary phenomenon. Men are there seen in a greater equality in point of fortune and intellect, or, in other words, more equal in their strength, than in any other country of the world, or in any age of which history has preserved the remembrance.' [10] However, although this egalitarianism was the foundation of American democracy it was not without an illiberal aspect. He observed that in 'the United States, the majority undertakes to supply a multitude of ready-made opinions for the use of individuals, who are thus relieved from the necessity of forming opinions of their own'.[11] The absence of social distinctions also encouraged men to compete with one another in the acquisition of wealth, but far from distinguishing one man from another the American's desire to amass a fortune 'gives to all their passions a sort of family likeness, and soon renders the survey of them exceedingly wearisome'.[12] In spite of the fact that in America there existed respect for the rule of law, and government responsible to the majority of the people for carrying out its mandate, there remains the fact that the voice of minorities carried little weight, and that the mass placed considerable pressure on the individual to conform to the prevailing life-style. Mill, in reviewing de Tocqueville's work, felt obliged to stress again his deeply held conviction that now 'as ever, the greatest problem in government is to prevent the strongest from becoming the only power; and repress the natural tendency of the instincts and passions of the ruling body to sweep away all barriers which are capable of resisting, even for a moment, their own tendencies'.[13]

In England the liberal reaction to the French Revolution was not so pronounced as that in France. Enthusiasm for national self-determination survived in the work of Wordsworth, Shelley and Byron. The romantics amongst the English liberals were the first foreigners to champion the cause of Spanish and Greek patriots against the French and Turkish oppressor. Wordsworth expressed the view in 1809 that Spanish resistance to Napoleon was conducted 'not for insulated privilege, but for the rights of human nature; not for temporal blessing, but for eternal happiness; not for the benefits of one nation; but for all mankind, and even for France herself'.[14]

Wordsworth, like Byron in the case of the struggle for Greek independence, held that the cause of the Spanish people must also be the cause of every liberal in the world. The eventual victory was inevitable. As Shelley conceived the future of liberalism in England, so Wordsworth and Byron conceived it in the world: its progress is not only 'necessary because it is just and ought to be, but necessary because it is inevitable and must be'.[15]

That the liberal cause was both universal and destined to be everywhere victorious became a prominent feature of nineteenth-century liberalism. Giuseppe Mazzini, originally regarded as a liberal for championing the cause of Italian independence, expressed the renewed spirit of optimism in a series of essays published between 1844 and 1858. These were collected under the title *The Duties of Man*. 'We improve,' he wrote, 'with the improvement of Humanity; nor without improvement of the whole can you hope that your own moral and material conditions will improve.'[16] The liberation of Italy from Austrian domination was as much the concern of Englishmen as Italians. There is, he believed, only one fundamental principle for all political and moral action:

> Ask yourselves whenever you do an action in the sphere of your country, or your family, if what I am doing were done by all and for all, would it advantage or injure Humanity? And if your conscience answers, It would injure Humanity, desist, even if it seems to you that an immediate advantage for your country or your family would ensue from your action.[17]

By the middle of the nineteenth century liberalism was as firmly committed to international support for national self-determination as it was to international free trade. Mill in *A Few Words on Non-Intervention*, published in 1859, spelt out the conditions under which this support should take a positive form. It was, he believed, wrong for liberals to seek to impose free institutions on those not themselves struggling to establish them. Those who did not appreciate their value were not ready to govern themselves, but those whose aspirations for self-government were denied by a foreign power ought to receive positive assistance in resisting this interference in their national affairs. In his *Considerations on Representative Government* Mill went so far as to assert that 'the boundaries of governments should coincide in the main with those of nationalities'.[18] The cause of representative government, we are told, cannot be separated from that of national self-determination. However, but a little later in the century, Acton saw fit to point out that although the creation of representative

institutions might require national independence, the achievement of national independence did not of itself necessarily lead to
the creation of democratic government. In his essay *Nationality*,
published in 1862, Acton observed that it was the spirit of
nationalism which led France under Napoleon to suppress the
aspiration for national independence elsewhere in Continental
Europe:

> It overrides the rights and wishes of the inhabitants, absorb-
> ing their divergent interests in a fictitious unity; sacrifices
> their several inclinations and duties to the higher claims of
> nationality, and crushes all natural rights and all established
> liberties for the purpose of vindicating itself.[19]

Acton's conclusion is that, contrary to first impressions, the
'theory of nationality, therefore, is a retrograde step in history'.[20]
After the Franco-German war of 1870 the course of European
history seemed, to liberals, to confirm this judgment.

The danger Acton detected in the rise of European nationalism
is similar to the danger de Staël and Constant detected in popular
self-government, and de Tocqueville and Mill in the cultural
domination of a homogeneous majority. All three made for
uniformity. The movements for popular government and
national self-determination were both progressive in so far as
they were destructive of despotism and feudal hierarchy, but they
were both reactionary in so far as they increased the danger of
intolerance towards minorities. Moreover all three developments
were related to one of the principal threats to the liberal ideal of
liberty in the nineteenth century. This threat is the bureaucratic
state. It took the place that royal despotism had occupied in the
eighteenth century.

For and Against Laissez-faire

One of the first to detect and oppose the intervention of the
modern state in social and economic affairs was Baron von
Humboldt. His work, *On the Limits of State Action*, written half
a century before its publication in 1852, attracted considerable

attention, including that of Mill. Von Humboldt portrayed the administrative state as the greatest single threat to the development of human potential. He argues that the 'true end of man . . . is the highest and most harmonious development of his powers to a complete and consistent whole'.[21] This cannot be achieved through the exercise of the power of the state. Where the power of the state is used to order the social and economic life of its subjects 'interference increases, the agents to which it is applied come to resemble each other, as do the results of their activity. And this is the very design which states have in view. They desire comfort, ease, tranquillity; and these are most readily secured to the extent that there is no clash of individualities. But what man does and must have in view is something quite different—it is variety and activity.' [22] It is as individual citizens, not as uniform subjects, that men have the best opportunity to develop their personal talents. The regulation of human relationships by the state diminishes the opportunity of every man to become a morally autonomous, useful and responsible member of his community.

Von Humboldt formed his political opinions in opposition to the development of the enlightened absolution of the Prussian bureaucracy. They were received and understood in rather different circumstances. By 1850, in Europe, and 1900, in America, industrialization, urbanization and increased population was accompanied by poverty, disease, ignorance, inhuman conditions of employment and periods of unemployment. Each of these developments invited an increase in legislation designed to protect the weaker members of a society in which competition between individuals determined relative standards of living. The majority of liberals feared that such intervention would undermine the economic foundation of society. It would destroy the proud independence of the working man and the entrepreneurial spirit of his employer. It was thought, for several decades, that no matter how humanitarian the inspiration behind legislation to regulate the terms of contract between employer and employee for the protection of the interests of the latter, it must seriously hamper the creation of wealth and diminish the working man's chance of a share of it. At the same time it must increase the power of the state and the numbers employed by it in unproductive labour. The prospect was demoralizing.

In many ways the ground was well prepared for the reception of von Humboldt's ideas long before the date of their delayed publication. As early as 1836 Richard Cobden had enthusiastically attacked the proposal that the state should regulate conditions of employment. He wrote:

> I yield to no man in the world (be he ever so stout an advocate of the Ten Hours' Bill) in a hearty good-will towards the great body of the working class; but my sympathy is not of that morbid kind which would lead me to despond over their future prospects. Nor do I partake of the spurious humanity which would indulge in an unreasonable kind of philanthropy at the expense of the great bulk of the community. Mine is that masculine species of charity which would lead me to instil in the minds of the labouring classes the love of independence, the privilege of self-respect, the disdain of being patronized or petted, the desire to accumulate, and the ambition to rise.[23]

Mill was rather more sympathetic to the proposal that the state assist those unable to help themselves, but in 1845 he was emphatic that all such assistance be calculated to set the recipients on their own feet as soon as possible:

> Of schemes destined specially to give them employment, or add to their comforts, it may be said, once and for all, that there is a simple test by which to judge them. Is the assistance of such a kind, and given in such a manner, as to render them ultimately independent of the continuance of similar assistance?[24]

For Herbert Spencer, who did more than any other single liberal writer to identify liberal doctrine with capitalism, as distinct from commercialism, even this was too much. In his most famous essay *The Man Versus the State*, published in 1884, he bitterly observed that 'the immense majority of the persons who wish to mitigate by law the miseries of the unsuccessful and the reckless, propose to do this in small measure at their own cost and mainly at the cost of others—sometimes with their assent but mostly without'.[25] Nothing, he believed, could be better designed to discourage the industrious from relying on their own initiative and to increase the numbers of those in the service of the state. It is simply a law of nature that the worker who cannot compete in the labour market, like the manufacturer who cannot compete in the market for goods, must make way for those who can. The same point was made with brutal frankness by Spencer's American counterpart, William Graham Sumner, in 1881. 'The law of the survival of the fittest was not made by man and cannot be abrogated by man. We can only, by interfering with it, produce the survival of the unfittest.'[26] Sumner was not afraid to accept the implications of this doctrine when it came to the concrete instance of the human tragedy ruthless competition entailed. 'A drunkard in the gutter,' he wrote in 1884, 'is just where he ought to be, according to the fitness of things. Nature has set up in him the process of decline and dissolution by which she removes things which have survived their usefulness.'[27]

The work of Spencer and Sumner is an approach to a turning point in the story of liberalism comparable with that approached by Sieyès and Mazzini. The course of the French Revolution and the rise of militant European nationalism, respectively, appear to have diminished the appeal that Sieyès and Mazzini might otherwise have had for later liberal writers. At least we can say that the cause of popular government and national self-determination received only qualified support from liberals writing at a later date. In the case of Spencer and Sumner, both in England and America, there was a decisive reaction against the kind of social Darwinism they had propagated. The spectacle of human misery and the prospect of class war presented by nineteenth-century capitalism was no more acceptable to the Christian liberal than had the excesses of the French Revolution proved acceptable to Constant or Prussian militarism to Acton.

In England the new direction to liberal thinking was given by Francis Montague, T. H. Green and Leonard Hobhouse. In

America Herbert Croly, John Dewey and Alfred Berle pointed the way. By the middle of this century John Maynard Keynes, Friedrich Hayek, Sir Isaiah Berlin and Sir Karl Popper had made a major contribution to liberal thinking in Britain. Across the Atlantic their peers are Joseph Schumpeter, Walter Lippman, Arthur Schlesinger Jr. and John Kenneth Galbraith. To begin with the emphasis, particularly in America, is on economic problems. In Europe, the preoccupation with the less attractive aspects of industrial society is made a secondary concern by the rise of totalitarian movements. It is not true to say that liberals in America have not interested themselves in Europe's political problems. America's involvement in two world wars, followed by her confrontation with international communism, destroyed the possibility of political insularity. Nevertheless, the depression and the New Deal are the major events in the history of liberal thought in America. This, perhaps, is less surprising than the fact that America has not produced more prominent contributors to the tradition than she has. It is difficult to think of American authors as influential as Locke, Smith, Mill and Spencer, even in America herself. The reason for this is probably the obvious one. The seventeenth- and eighteenth-century battle against divine right and feudalism, and the nineteenth-century struggle with nationalism and socialism, took place in Europe. During this century, in spite of the impact of the depression, America did not go bankrupt. Moreover, she did not suffer anarchy, revolution, civil war or defeat and occupation. She came in fact to dominate, in political, economic and military terms, a world which suffered all of these catastrophes. There has not in consequence, in living memory, been the occasion for liberals seriously to question the American way of life. The McCarthy campaign, the Vietnam war and racial riots have not led to a rejection of the current application of liberal principles or of the values liberals respect. They have called for the more vigorous pursuit or reaffirmation of them. It is not going too far to say that the American negro, who, before all others, might be expected violently to reject American society, has asked for little more than the opportunity to get on in it. The country has its famous critics, Eric Frömm, Noam

Chomsky and Herbert Marcuse amongst them, but they are not liberals, and they have heralded little more than campus disturbances. For all of its failings American society has not produced the kind of oppression which has occasioned the most famous articulations of the liberal disposition in Europe. Including the history of the negro and the Indian, from Jefferson to Kennedy, nothing like the horrors of Stalin's Russia and Hitler's Germany have appeared in America. In his *Letter from a Birmingham Jail*, published in 1963, Martin Luther King eloquently affirmed his faith in the effectiveness of civil disobedience as a means of securing the American negro his civil rights. And, in spite of King's tragic death, the advance of the negro's cause would suggest that this faith was not entirely misplaced. But it is inconceivable that civil disobedience could have proved effective against Stalin or Hitler. The voice of liberalism has usually been raised in protest, and if it has not been heard to say anything dramatically new in America's recent history it may well be because, from a liberal point of view, the occasion has not arisen.

As suggested, in America the principal contributions to liberal thinking have been made to economic theory and to the solution of the social problems generated by industrial society. Even here, however, English authors led the way. The fertile ground for ideological confrontation is social and political conflict. During the latter half of the nineteenth century it took the form of class conflict, and as Marx observed, the country in which the struggle was most acute is England. During the depression of the 1880s it became desperately obvious that something was radically wrong. The pursuit of liberal objectives had not resulted in the kind of society anticipated. In 1885 Montague assessed the problem in the following terms:

> The most celebrated reformers have been those who abridged the exorbitant power of classes, corporations, and sects; who liberated truth, liberated education, liberated religion; who very nearly secured to all men the employment of equal civil and political rights ... leave man, they

99

said, to the monitions of his own unprejudicial reason, of his own warm and kindly instincts. These will guide him aright whilst states and churches can only lead him astray.[28]

However, the facts, as perceived by Montague, suggested that the liberated individual had not become a superior moral being, and the institutions he has reformed had not guaranteed universal happiness. On the contrary:

> At the present day political and social perfection seem nearly as remote as ever . . . enlarged individual freedom has done for human greatness or human happiness only a very small part of what its noblest advocates expected.[29]

Montague found that the creation of a competitive economy had promoted an intense and degrading competition between men destructive of their 'finer human feelings'. Instead of promoting social harmony it had promoted class conflict and facilitated exploitation. In short, the very circumstances in which we may expect the principal rival of liberal ideas, the doctrine of socialism, to have the widest appeal. Montague believed that adherence to the doctrine of 'modern socialism expresses the practical revolt against the doctrine of negative freedom'.[30] It was now apparent that liberals were wedded to an archaic conception of human experience in which 'intellectual life is reduced to a series of sensations, the moral life to a series of impulses, and society to a collection of individuals'.[31] Mill, for example, had completely failed to appreciate the extent to which man is a social being. 'Mr Mill could hardly have accepted the distinction between self-regarding and social acts, had it not grown naturally out of the social theory current amongst his predecessors.'[32] One has only to look at the appalling conditions in which the majority of working people live to realize that society, through the agency of the state, must accept responsibility for the moral, cultural, and material standards of modern life:

> The philosophers who hold that in our day all grown-up men and women can attain their normal development without any other assistance than is afforded by unlimited

competition and unrestrained discussion, must have either a very narrow experience or a very weak imagination.[33]

It is evident from Green's *Lectures on the Principles of Political Obligation*, first delivered in 1879, that independently he had reached the same conclusion. The liberal belief that the state ought not to attempt to enforce moral beliefs and regulate the economic activity of the individual had been formed at a time when the chief threat to individual liberty was royal despotism. As such, it was perfectly intelligible to Green. The attitude embodied, he believed, the sound principles that men can neither be compelled to be moral beings nor made free by the attempt to direct their employment. Nevertheless, the principles do not prescribe that the state may not usefully remove hindrances to man's moral development, or that the state may not take steps to prevent the exploitation of a worker unable to secure a fair wage. According to Green those who maintain that the principles do proscribe such intervention are wholly mistaken and the existence of gross immorality and widespread poverty is proof of the fact. The truth is that in its original form the liberal theory of freedom, no matter how successful it has been in securing individual rights in the past, 'now tends to become obstructive, because in fact advancing civilization brings with it more and more interference with the liberty of the individual to do as he likes, and this theory affords a reason for resisting all positive reforms, all reforms which involve an action of the state in the way of promoting conditions favourable to moral life'.[34] It cannot be denied, Green affirms, that in so far as society has a moral purpose it is to facilitate the development of its members as moral beings. Therefore, no reasonable objection can be brought against an exercise of the authority of government and the power of the state to further this objective.

Hobhouse also found Mill's objection to the legal regulation of any but what he conceived to be 'other-regarding' actions to be ill-founded. Along with Montague and Green he took the view that in so far as 'Mill rested his case on the distinction between self-regarding actions and actions that affect others, he was still dominated by the older individualism'.[35] We can now see that the right to liberty 'rests not on the claim of A to be let alone by B, but on the duty of B to treat A as a rational being'.[36] The government of a civil society has the responsibility of proscribing actions which inhibit the development of moral personality. The 'function of state coercion is to override individual coercion, and, of course, coercion exercised by any association of individuals within the state'.[37] It has, for example, the responsibility of protecting the working man's right to combine with his fellows to secure a living wage. Since, to a very large extent, the accumulation of private wealth is less the product of individual initiative and sacrifice than of the institutions and legal arrangements of society, it is only right that the state should, via progressive taxation, appropriate part of that wealth with a view to helping those not in a position to help themselves. The ultimate purpose of society is not the creation of private fortunes by a minority. It is the welfare of all of its members. The education of the young, help for the aged and infirm, the housing of the poor and the provision of work for a fair wage are the legitimate concern of the state. At the turn of the century Hobhouse believed that the greatest advance to be made in securing the liberty of the individual was in the direction of greater social and economic equality.

Reflecting on the development of the English legal system in the nineteenth century Albert Dicey advanced the thesis, in *Law and Public Opinion in England*, that between 1825 and 1870 the chief object of law reform had been to increase the area of individual self-determination. Thereafter it had been less concerned with liberty than to implement a policy designed to satisfy a notion of social justice. The transition was one from a policy of laissez-faire to a policy of collectivism. The development was a response to the social and economic circumstances encouraged by the earlier objective. Logically, however, Dicey conceived the two policies to be incompatible, and it seems likely that Montague, Green and Hobhouse would be inclined to agree with this judgment. There had been a change of policy, a gradual change, but a definite change. In their opinion what had been a correct application of liberal principles would now be an incorrect application, not a different application to that which they pre-scribed. In short, after 1870, the position of Mill and Spencer was erroneous. By 1939, however, it was apparent to Barker, writing with hindsight, that no such impasse had been reached, and that the dispute between the advocates of individualism and collecti-vism originated in a misunderstanding:

> Generally the whole of the nineteenth century, far from being divided into two different parts, was a century of a single and harmonious process; a process of the extension of personal rights, which may be called individualism, but a process entailing, at the same time, an extension which may be called by the name of collectivism, but is really and in fact the consequence and the other side of the extension of personal rights which is called by the name of indi-vidualism.[38]

As far as Barker is concerned one major controversy within the liberal camp was at an end, and, as it happened, his conclusion is in accord with changed opinion within the Liberal Party at the outbreak of World War II.

Whatever may have been the effect of the work of Montague, Green and Hobhouse on the climate of political opinion in England the leadership of the Liberal Party provided by Lloyd George was, in the eyes of contemporary liberal ideologists, altogether more radical than that provided by Gladstone. Keynes, for example, considered that by 1925 liberal policies were more compatible with the new thinking than with the slogans of the party. Addressing the Liberal Economic Summer School he observed that in England we 'have changed, by sensible degrees, our philosophy of economic life, our notions of what is reason-able and what is tolerable; and we have done this without changing our copy-book maxims. Hence our tears and troubles.'[39] What was required in England was the re-education of the members of the Liberal Party rather than a rejection of the new leadership. But in America the situation was entirely different. Here the economic and political theory of the minimum state was entirely in accord with political talk and practice. In economic terms Sumner's capitalistist ethic was not directly challenged by 'respectable' theorists until after World War I. In political terms the individualism expressed in Thoreau's essay *Civil Disobedience*, published in 1849, remains attractive to this day.

As in England, it was unanticipated economic developments rather than a change in the intellectual climate that provoked the American reaction. As America entered the Great Depression, John Dewey observed that most of 'those who are engaged in the outward work of production and distribution of economic commodities have no share—imaginative, intellectual, emotional—in directing the activities in which they physically participate'.[40] Vast industrial corporations treated their employees as a factor of production comparable with capital investment, and, for their part, the employees laboured purely for their wage in constant fear of dismissal. It was difficult to perceive in this the realization of the liberal dream:

> The spiritual factor of our tradition, equal opportunity and free association and intercommunication, is obscured and crowded out . . . Instead of the development of individualities which it prophetically set forth, there is a perversion of the whole ideal of individualism to conform to the practices of a pecuniary culture. It has become the source and justification of inequalities and oppressions.[41]

Something of the same spirit permeates *The Vital Center: The Politics of Freedom*, published by Arthur Schlesinger Jr. in 1949. Following Keynes, Schlesinger asks for a certain standard of welfare and level of employment to be guaranteed by the state. This is claimed to be desirable not only for economic reasons, but also for the health of America's democratic institutions. The fear that American society will destroy itself unless what are judged its more inhuman aspects are countered is a persistent theme in liberal writing. Herbert Croley, for example, whose work, *The Promise of American Life*, appeared as early as 1909, observed that uncontrolled private enterprise tends to eliminate the conditions under which it first appeared and flourished. The accumulation of capital in fewer and fewer hands, which is the consequence of unlimited competition, effectively removes the opportunity for all but a small minority to compete at all. Unless the American public can bring themselves to accept that the size of private fortunes and industrial empires will have to be limited, they will have to accept that economic freedom is a thing of the past. In 1932 Adolf Berle published *The Modern Corporation and Private Property* in which he expresses a similar anxiety. His thesis is that the separation of management control from the ownership of stock in the modern corporation has led to the largest part of the profit going to those who cannot influence its policy or increase its efficiency. The result is that the profit motive cannot work effectively. Unless the state intervenes to direct a larger share of the profit to the workers and management of the modern corporation we may confidently expect economic decline. Another twist to the now familiar argument was given by Schumpeter in 1942. He drew attention to the fact that the industrial corporation, formed to reap the benefits of economy of scale, had significantly reduced the opportunity for the exercise of private initiative. In what had been taken to be economic progress work tends to become 'depersonalized and automatized. Bureau and committee work tends to replace individual action.' [42] Far from encouraging private enterprise the 'capitalist process pushes into the background all those institutions, the institutions of property and free contracting in particular, that expressed the needs and ways of the truly private economic activity'.[43]

The problem according to Galbraith, the most recent American liberal ideologist with an international reputation, originates in the long-held belief that all man's needs could be met by increased production. In spite of the obvious facts that the quality of urban life, and the opportunities for the majority of Americans to enjoy the cultural and physical benefits of increased wealth were in decline, opinion in favour of increased production prevailed. The demoralizing effects of the factory assembly line, the pollution of the environment and the waste involved in excessive consumption are ignored. The wealth that might have been devoted to public health, art, education and welfare is squandered in the form of built-in obsolescence, the elaborate packaging of goods and pressure salesmanship. The satisfaction of the resulting artificial demand is financed by easy credit, and the employment it creates leads to the further abuse of the working man unable to escape the squalor and violence of urban and factory life. Galbraith's conclusion is that 'we are guided, in part, by ideas that are relevant to another world; and as a result we do many things that are unnecessary, some that are unwise, and a few that are insane'.[44] The opinions of Dewey, Schumpeter, Schlesinger and Galbraith concur with those of Cohen, whose book *The Faith of a Liberal* appeared in 1946:

> Traditionally, liberalism has been conceived as a form of individualism. Liberalism in economics has been associated with opposition to collective controls over production and distribution. In politics liberalism has been historically associated with the supremacy of individual rights. Neither of these beliefs has a very bright future . . . the essentials of the liberal attitude are entirely compatible with a belief that the growing interdependence of men in an industrial age calls for an increasing scope of governmental activity in fields once left to private charity and private initiative.[45]

It is possible to consider the leadership of the Democratic party by Kennedy and Johnson as representing this, the new spirit of liberalism in America, but the fact remains that nothing like the shift in political opinion noted by Keynes in England occurred across the Atlantic. And this is spite of the fact that in England the Liberal Party contracted under the strain of reluctantly accepting the implications of collectivism. After 1918 much of the electoral support previously given to the English Liberal Party went to the Labour Party, and by the outbreak of World War II the Liberal Party had ceased to be a major political force.

The development in liberal thinking represented by Montague, Green and Hobhouse in England, and by Dewey, Schlesinger, Galbraith and Cohen in America, made it possible to speak of a brand of ideological thought as liberal-socialism. Croce, for example, perhaps the most distinguished of Italian liberals, considered it perfectly reasonable for the Italian of 'liberal conscience, to support measures and regulations which the theorist of abstract economy classify as socialist . . . (and) to speak of "liberal socialism", as . . . in a beautiful English eulogy and apology for liberalism by Hobhouse'.[46] This development, however, was paralleled by the emergence of what came to be termed liberal-conservatism, to be found in the works of Bagehot, Maine, Hirst, Martin, Ortega y Gasset, Lippmann, Friedman, Hayek, de Jouvenal, Popper, Talmon and Berlin. It grew out of the liberal reaction to the French Revolution and the granting of the vote to the working man. It is strongly opposed to the doctrine of socialism. It developed in bitter opposition to the rise of twentieth-century totalitarian movements in Russia, Germany and Italy. Liberal-socialism and liberal-conservatism were never entirely independent. Croce, for example, spanned the two, but many adhered to one or the other. In England, it might be said that, ideologically, the Liberal Party fell between the two stools.

Socialism and the Rise of Totalitarianism

The immediate occasion for the voice of liberal-conservatism to be heard in England was the extension of the franchise in 1867 and 1884, and the steady growth in the power of trade union organization towards the end of the century. Together these two developments placed in the hands of the working man a power to influence political decisions which had previously been the monopoly of those who regarded themselves as his social superiors. Walter Bagehot expressed the fear to which this change gave rise as early as 1867 in his popular work *The English Constitution*:

> Of all our political dangers the greatest I conceived is that . . . both our political parties will bid for the support of the working man; that both of them will promise to do as he likes . . . And, on the other hand, my imagination conjures up a contrary danger. I can conceive that questions being raised which, if continually agitated, would combine the working men as a class together, the higher orders might

have to consider whether they would concede the measures that would settle such questions, or whether they would risk the effect of the working men's combination.[47]

This middle-class fear of the consequences of the emancipation of the working man was closely linked with the belief that his political organization would lead to a vast increase in the power of the state. Sir Henry Maine made this analysis one of the central themes of his book *Popular Government*, published in 1886. He believed himself a witness of the emergence of 'the omnipotent democratic state . . . which has at its absolute disposal everything which individual men value, their property, their persons, and their independence . . . the state which may make laws for its subjects ordaining what they shall drink or eat, and in what way they shall spend their earnings . . . and which, if the effect on human motives is what it may be expected to be, may force us to labour in it when the older incentives to toil have disappeared'.[48] Maine seriously believed that European civilization 'may yet be launched into space and find its last affinities in silence and cold'.[49] He did not abandon the liberal belief in the possibility of human progress, but the old optimism was gone, and, for all but the most stout-hearted, the course of European history in the first half of the twentieth century did little to revive it.

Maine's proved to be one of the most prophetic of liberal utterances in the late nineteenth century. But his was not a lone voice. It is amongst the most individual, but there is also the chorus of Lord Thomas Erskine May, William Lilly and Sir William Lecky. Theirs, however, was a less original interpretation of events. The intellectual steel in their arguments had been tempered by Spencer. They merely used it to belabour the arguments and policies of the socialists who represented, in their eyes, all the evil tendencies of the age. According to May, under socialism 'no man is to profit by his own strength, abilities, or industry; but is to minister to the wants of the weak, the stupid and the idle'.[50] Lilly discerned that it is certain 'that the very foundation of socialism is the doctrine of absolute power of numerical majorities'.[51] And Lecky concluded that popular

government inevitably leads to a 'weakening of private enterprise and philanthropy; a lowered sense of individual responsibility; diminished love of freedom; the creation of an array of
officials, regulating in all departments the affairs of life; the
formation of a state of society in which vast multitudes depend
for their subsistence on the bounty of the state'.[52] Lecky found it
incredible that men who claimed to be liberal had argued that
political power should be given to what he understood to be 'the
poorest, the most ignorant, the most incapable, who are necessarily, the most numerous. The day will come,' he reflected,
'when it will appear one of the strangest facts in the history of
human folly that such a theory was regarded as liberal and
progressive.'[53]

In the twentieth century the voice of liberal-conservatism
became progressively more strident. It did not make a major
contribution to the debate on the origins of World War I;
German militarism was characterized more as an aspect of the
autocratic state than a mass movement and this interpretation
was not peculiar to liberal-conservatism. But in the years following, the coming to power of communist, national socialist and
fascist parties and their creation of the totalitarian state fell neatly
within the analysis the liberal-conservatives claimed as their own.
In his *History of European Liberalism*, de Ruggiero observed
that in the twentieth century the course of events was increasingly
unfavourable to liberal values:

> Lack of education on the part of the masses whom a fiat has
> raised to the position of sovereignty; the necessity of
> making oneself acceptable to a body of electors untrained in
> politics, which leads to the display of the least creditable
> abilities calculated to subserve the lower interests of the
> state ... all these circumstances widen the gulf between the
> actual majority and the minority of representatives, and
> threaten to make of democracy a tyranny over the many in
> the interests of the few.[54]

In 1930 the American liberal E. D. Martin observed the course
of European history with profound misgivings. It seemed that the

intellectual élite, 'that attained the life of reason', were powerless to preserve the liberty necessary to cultural advance in the face of the demands of the ignorant masses:

> To the majority liberty has been and still is, the removal of restraints to mass action. They can be led to co-operate with liberals in resisting the tyranny which a ruling class may impose upon them from without; but they seem to be defenceless against their own forms of tyranny of the mass.[55]

It was the prospect of this tyranny that inspired Ortega y Gasset to write *The Revolt of the Masses*, one of the few Spanish political texts to gain international recognition. He expressed the fear that, astutely misled, the masses will readily provide the support necessary to make the power of the state unlimited. The consequences for civilization must, he believed, prove disastrous. Totalitarianism destroys the creative power of a culture through 'the absorption of all spontaneous social effort by the state, that is to say, of spontaneous historical action, which in the long run sustains, nourishes and impels human destinies'.[56] In 1935, five years after the appearance of y Gasset's book, totalitarianism was a reality in Russia, Germany and Italy. Francis Hirst confessed that what had been deemed impossible had happened. The political victories of liberalism were being reversed.

> Two centuries of emancipation have been followed by two decades of reaction. In several great and small countries free visitations have been trampled underfoot; criticism has been stifled; the press has been enslaved; trade has been trammelled by innumerable restrictions, and whole nations are being deprived of their economic liberties as well as of their rights.[57]

Hirst found it exceedingly difficult to understand how the value of personal liberty could be depreciated and the arguments for democracy discounted in Europe, the continent in which they had originated. He was obliged to conclude that the doctrine of liberalism, formed in an age of reason, was now received in an age of irrationalism. It must be recognized that it may well be the case that liberal arguments cannot convince those who are attracted by the mysticism and romanticism of the new doctrines. In which case the democratic nations must prove their superiority by actions rather than words.

> When, for example, a Mussolini, a Hitler or a Stalin consigns liberals to gaol or death, or pours contempt upon liberty and liberalism . . . it is not enough to make a theoretical answer. It is necessary to show that . . . there is more patriotism, more harmony and more solidarity in a self-governing nation than in a subject race.[58]

Lippmann, observing Europe from across the Atlantic, shared Hirst's belief that it was futile to attempt to persuade fascist and communist régimes to show any respect for liberal values. One has only to attend to what is said by their leaders to realize that between the democratic and totalitarian way of life no common understanding is possible:

> The fascist conception of life accepts the individual only in so far as his interests coincide with those of the state. Does communism accept the individual on any other terms? Does it recognize any right to labour, to possess property, to think, to believe and to speak—which does not coincide with the interests of the State? It cannot.[59]

World War II was, from the liberal point of view, fought for ideological reasons. The issue was clear-cut and the outcome decisive. The forces of democracy and civilization triumphed over those of tyranny and barbarism. But totalitarianism was not entirely destroyed. National socialism and fascism were defeated, if not spent forces, but both within the states of the liberal victors, and in the form of the Soviet Union, the threat from communism was greater than before. Croce, writing in a country with an active communist party, frequently wrote to dispel the belief that, in the Soviet Union, the dream of a communist society was being made a reality. Far from a withering away of the Soviet state there had been 'an increase of state activity, centralizing and regulating to its own tastes every occupation and every thought, and turning even art and poetry into political propaganda'.[60] During the two decades following World War II an intense battle was fought between liberal and communist ideologists. The so-called 'cold war' of the confrontation of American and Soviet power in Europe provided the occasion for the last and perhaps the most vigorous display of the liberal ideological tradition. To its exponents it seemed that both from without and within the democratic states the communist threat was the greatest ever to endanger the way of life approved by liberals.

It ought never to be forgotten, Hayek warned his readers in *The Road to Serfdom*, that national socialism had its roots in the socialist ideal of a planned economy, and such is the support for collectivist measures in Britain that it may yet prove the case that she won the war but lost the peace. The danger is familiar:

> British strength, British character, and British achievements are to a great extent the result of a cultivation of the spontaneous. But almost all the traditions and institutions in which British moral genius has formed its most characteristic expression, and which in turn have moulded the national character and the moral climate of England, are those which the progress of collectivism and its inherently centralistic tendencies are progressively destroying.[61]

Hayek considered the English working class to be the unwitting victims of a conspiracy to deprive them of hard-won liberties in exchange for the illusory benefits of a planned economy. It is doubtful 'whether the majority of English workmen will in the end thank the intellectuals among their leaders who have presented them with a socialist doctrine which endangers their personal freedom'.[62] But the danger was, he thought, that by the time they realized they had exchanged the impersonal discipline of the market for the personal dictatorship of a few individuals, they would no longer have recourse to parliamentary methods to control their doctrinaire leaders. Hayek regards a competitive economy as indispensable to a free society. He believes that the 'guiding principle, that a policy of freedom for the individual is the only truly progressive policy, remains as true today as it was in the nineteenth century'.[63]

Hayek taught for some years at the University of Chicago. His contribution to liberalism is similar to that expounded at that time by his colleague there, Milton Friedman. In his major work, *Capitalism and Freedom*, Friedman restates the orthodox view that capitalism preserves freedom, because it divides economic from political power, thereby creating the essential counter-balance absent in centralized government.

The thesis that totalitarianism came into being through the propagation of an attractive but wholly false understanding of man's past and potential, was taken further in 1945 and 1957 in Popper's *The Open Society and its Enemies* and *The Poverty of Historicism*. By attacking those he regarded as the intellectual ancestors of totalitarian aspirations Popper sought to dismiss the claim that, on the basis of their understanding of change, social engineering can radically improve the human condition. He does not explain how it is that Plato, Hegel and Marx are responsible for totalitarianism, or how an attack on their works will save us from its proliferation. Nevertheless, in so far as his studies provide ample opportunity to denigrate ideologies which rival liberalism they serve their purpose. Popper's objective is exhortation not explanation. He urges us to defend our liberal values 'by defending and strengthening those democratic institutions upon which freedom, and with it progress, depends'.[64]

With Hayek and Popper liberal ideology reaffirmed its traditional intellectual sophistication. This has been sustained by Bertrand de Jouvenel in *On Power*, Jacob Talmon in *The Origins of Totalitarian Democracy* and Sir Isaiah Berlin in *Two Concepts of Liberty*. The man in the street may not have received the message but students of political philosophy throughout the English speaking world must by now be familiar with it. Once again they have been told:

The will of democratic power goes by the name of general. It crushes each individual beneath the weight of the sum of

113

> the individuals represented by it; it oppresses each private interest in the name of a general interest which is incarnate in itself.[65]

> Modern totalitarian democracy is a dictatorship ... based on an ideology and the enthusiasm of the masses, it is the outcome of the synthesis between the eighteenth-century idea of the natural order and the Rousseauist idea of popular fulfilment and self-expression.[66]

> The common assumption of these thinkers [Rousseau, Hegel and Marx prominent amongst them] ... is that the rational ends of our 'true' motives must coincide, or be made to coincide, however violently our poor, ignorant, desire-ridden, passionate, empirical selves may cry out against this process.[67]

Throughout the nineteenth and the twentieth centuries liberal theorists have persistently attacked ideas which justify the suppression of individual freedom by the nation, the state, the industrial corporation and the totalitarian party. They have constantly affirmed that progress is the product of individual effort and creativity. In the words of the political scientist James Bryce: 'Nothing is more vital to national progress than the spontaneous development of individual character, and that free play of intellect which is independent of current prejudice, examines everything by the light of reason and history, and fearlessly defends unpopular opinions.'[68] The threats to individual liberty were new, but the danger they represent is the same danger that liberals have always feared, the danger inherent in the arbitrary exercise of power. As Ramsey Muir put it in 1933, 'the price of liberty is eternal watchfulness; because when men get power into their hands they nearly always abuse it'.[69]

'In the early stages of society,' May affirmed in 1877, 'superstition and ignorance naturally prevailed; and the people were unfitted for the functions and privileges of freedom. Accordingly, we find them everywhere under the rule of kings, priests and nobles ... As European society advanced, heroic and heaven-born kings were generally succeeded by aristocracies; who in their turn, were constrained to share their power with the people, or to yield it to a democracy.' [70] For May, and his fellow-liberals, this, the story of human progress, is commensurate with the history of liberalism. The values enshrined in the democratic way of life are liberal values:

> The highest ideal of a democracy is that which secures to every citizen equality before the law, freedom of person, freedom in the family, freedom of conscience, freedom of opinion, freedom of speech, freedom of trade, freedom of labour, freedom of property, freedom of action when not injurious to the state or to society, in a share in the election of his rulers, and in the making of the laws by which he is governed, and in the rating of taxes which he is called upon to contribute: which provides that the enlightened will of the majority shall be the rule of all, while none shall be restrained, but for the general good; which, continuing the strength of a whole people, has for its first objective, security for the rights and liberties of every member of the state.[71]

And, as Croce has it:

> Concrete liberal institutions are the *ad hoc* products of political genius inspired by liberty, or, what comes to the same, of liberal genius equipped with political prudence. To keep this genius alive in a people is the supreme duty, but it must not be imagined that the majority of men can cultivate it consciously. To do so requires depth of feeling and power of intellectual synthesis found only in the ranks of the élite, who are devoted to the ideal.[72]

Without exception, every liberal writer whose work has been quoted in this chapter assumes that he belonged to an international intellectual aristocracy whose duty it is to civilize the world. They believe that man's progress constitutes the enduring testament to the power of ideas to shape human lives.

The liberal's understanding of progress presupposes that,

correctly used, the concepts justice, freedom and equality help us to see the essential differences between feudal and civil society. They refer to features of human relationships more or less absent in the former and fundamental to the latter. History shows that to the extent that constitutional government replaced hereditary kingship, and citizenship hierarchical feudal status, to that extent the enjoyment of justice, freedom and equality became a reality. Liberals by and large have not appreciated that the concepts of justice, freedom and equality may be applied equally well to different forms of society. A society is not simply one kind of human relationship defined in law. Provided that those who enjoy equal rights under a body of law are treated equally, by those whose responsibility it is to administer that law, we may reasonably claim that in any historical society, they have been treated justly and that their freedom has been protected. It is not the case that the ranks of feudal society were unequal in the possession of rights, because they possessed different rights. And it is not true that the members of a civil society derive equal benefit from their rights, because they possess the same rights. In both the feudal and civil form of legal association the different treatment of men in the same legal category may equally well occasion injustice and an infringement of freedom, and in both societies men may fail to live as well as they might. Moreover, although liberals have correctly perceived that an enemy of liberty is arbitrary government, they have been mistaken in believing that arbitrary government is a form of government, and not the abuse of any form of government. As Hobbes shows, there is, for example, no necessary connection between absolute hereditary monarchy and tyranny. It was not until liberal expectations of democracy were disappointed, in so far as it proved to be the case that the offices of this form of government might as readily be abused as those of any other, that it was apparent that justice, freedom and equality were not to be guaranteed, let alone increased, by constitutional changes. The discovery was unwelcome, and Acton, amongst others, chose to sidestep its implications for his belief in progress by affirming that the classical, medieval and modern ideas of justice, freedom and equality are different, but to the extent that they have changed they have changed for the better. As a result we may rest assured that at least our failure to live up to our standards is a failure to live up to a higher standard than that of our ancestors. However, the concepts of justice, freedom and equality, as distinct from the practical implication of their application in different forms of society, cannot change any more than the concept of house can change because the form of houses has changed. Moreover, it is not the case, as many liberals have assumed, that because the true meanings of concepts have been more clearly seen, or superior concepts discovered, that the form of society has been changed, let alone improved. The form of societies, that is their legal rules, have been changed because the historical circumstances, the conditions of human life, have changed. But the laws of modern society are no more true laws than the modern application of the concepts justice, freedom and equality are the correct, as distinct from possible, applications.

The liberal concept of society is simply a different application of the concept to that which preceded it. It is not a better, or more true, concept of what a society is or should be—a society, for example, more in accord with natural law. The claim that a civil society is a superior form of society, because it is more in accordance with an absolute standard, is vacuous, unless it can be demonstrated what that standard prescribes independent of historical circumstances. This cannot be done without assuming that ideological concepts are demonstrable truths. For example, before the American John Rawls, in his book *Justice*, can demonstrate that the civil society of liberalism is the just society he has first to take the liberal concept of man as an autonomous individual as an a-historic or self-evident truth.[73] That the medieval mind did not grasp this 'truth' is part of the liberal theory of progress, but it does not follow that the medieval man had a defective concept of justice, and that there was, in consequence, greater injustice suffered by the members of his society. In every society there may be injustice, subjection and inequality, just as there may be disorder and unhappiness. A civil society is not the just, free and equal society, and it is not the society in which men

Liberalism

are necessarily peaceful and happy. Rather it is a form of society, within which a consistent and appropriate application of the concepts of justice, freedom and equality is possible, and in which men are peaceful when they have reason to be and happy when they truthfully say they are.

However, for the liberal to admit that there is no necessary connection between what he claims to be the true principles of politics, and the value of the experience of those whose legal order he believes those principles ought to shape, does expose at least three of his most basic beliefs. They are, one, the belief that he belongs to an intellectual élite, whose duty it is to discover the true meaning of what Thomas Weldon has called the 'vocabulary of politics'; [74] two, the belief that it is his business to educate the masses both in the correct use of that vocabulary, and in the practice of politics whereby what that vocabulary signifies as good may be created and that which is evil destroyed; and three, the belief that he is engaged in correcting the errors of his predecessors and revising their tradition of discourse. The history of liberal thinking is the history of the many contributions to a tradition of ideological thought, not the history of its progressive refinement. Liberalism and political truth, whatever that is, have not been shown to be synonymous.

5 The Foundations and Logic of Liberal Arguments

Although liberal doctrines have not been proved to be the true principles of political practice it has been the objective of many liberal writers to demonstrate that their political conclusions logically follow from either incontestable metaphysical foundations or indisputable factual evidence. Throughout the history of liberalism there has been a constant pursuit of an irrefutable truth upon which to build liberal arguments. Although developments in intellectual life, political practice and the circumstances of its conduct have defied liberal expectations, leading liberal thinkers to abandon old opinions in favour of new ones, this has not deterred them from the search for certainty. At different times it has appeared that the object of the search had been found in the conclusions of a famous theologian, historian, philosopher or scientist. What is more, liberals have themselves, in their capacity as theologians, historians, philosophers and scientists, made contributions to the understanding of experience which they, and their fellow ideologists, have deemed to be of political significance. Milton as a theologian, Acton as an historian, Kant as a philosopher, Priestley as a physical scientist and Smith and Spencer as social scientists each believed that their professional work substantiated their political belief. And, in the case of Locke's theology, Spencer's sociology, Mill's utilitarianism and Green's idealism the connection between the larger framework of their understanding and their political ideas not only made those ideas more acceptable to them, it helped to make the framework more popular. The connection has attracted attention to intellectual developments that might otherwise have passed unnoticed by practical men anxious to change the world. It would be to neglect an important aspect of ideological liberalism if we failed to examine the part played by the claim that certain first principles and facts underwrite the liberal message. More important, this neglect would involve our dismissing out of hand the possibility that a leading liberal theorist had proved that his particular brand of liberalism differed from all other formulations of the doctrine in alone compelling right-thinking or honest men to accept a political programme or reform. In other words, that it is the standard by which all other liberal theories are to be judged a success or failure. To avoid this omission it is proposed, in this chapter, to examine the relationship between the metaphysics and political ideas of Locke, Mill, Spencer and Green. The object of this exercise is to discover whether or not it can be said that any one of these major liberal theorists has demonstrated that his political conclusions are the only ones that can be said to follow from relevant and indisputable facts and theories.

To accomplish this task it is proposed to concentrate on four works, *The Second Treatise of Government*, *Representative Government*, *The Man Versus the State* and *Lectures on the Principles of Political Obligation*. Locke and Spencer have been particularly influential in America, Mill and Green in England. The works in question have been selected, first, because they are all famous liberal writings, secondly, because their arguments systematically proceed from first principles to practice and thirdly, because the prescribed principles and practice are distinct in each case. Now it has to be admitted that Locke's work differs from that of his nineteenth-century successors in a way that they do not differ from one another. This fact is connected with changes in the intellectual climate during the years which divide Locke from Mill, Spencer and Green. What Locke has to say about the form and purpose of government is unrelated to progress. For Locke, the basic conditions of life and human nature are unalterable; Mill, Spencer and Green believe that they evolve. For the purpose of this chapter this difference may be ignored. It does not oblige us to conclude that the methodology of Mill, Spencer and Green is one and the same thing, or that there is no relationship between the structure of their arguments and that of Locke. There is a connection between all four other than the one afforded by the tradition of political discourse to which they all belong. It is to be found in the logic of arguments designed to effect a transition from theory to practice; arguments of the kind we are now concerned to explore.

Locke's Theological Argument in 'The Second Treatise of Government'

In his *First Treatise* Locke attacked the doctrine of divine right as defended by Sir Robert Filmer in his polemic *Patriarcha*. In his *Second Treatise* he outlined what he took to be the 'True Original Extent and End of Civil Government'. The purpose of civil society, we are told, is to facilitate a life more in accordance with God's design than we could otherwise hope to live. In the order of God's creation man has the rights and duties prescribed by natural law. 'Reason, which is the law' forbids our destruction of 'the life, liberty, health, limb or goods of another'.[1] The rights to which we have title as human beings do not permit our behaving as beasts. We may not oblige another man to submit to our arbitrary will, destroy ourselves or that which is owned by, or is of use to others, and we have the duty to punish those who disregard this ruling. The purpose of human life, whether it be lived in a state of nature or in a civil society, is the service of God. Men are 'all the servants of one sovereign Master, sent into the world by His order, and about His business. They are His property, whose workmanship they are, made to last during His, not another's pleasure ...'[2]

Now the state of nature in which God originally placed man is not one in which he is deprived of the company of his fellow human beings. It is no more an a-social than an a-moral condition. God having 'made man such a creature, that, in His own judgment, it was not good for him to be alone, put him under strong obligations of necessity, conscience, and inclination to drive him into society, as well as fitted him with understanding and language to continue and enjoy it'.[3] However, although men, as of necessity, are driven to seek the company of their fellows, they are not irresistibly driven to harm them. The state of nature is not one of material deprivation in which only the fittest can expect to survive. For all those who are prepared to labour there are sufficient resources to maintain themselves and their families. That which belongs to no other any man may appropriate for his use, but he may not, on grounds of want, any more than of right, deprive others of their lives or possessions unless he is himself the victim of such an attack. When this occurs he is in a state of war rather than a state of nature with the aggressor. In this state men are entitled to kill in self-defence, but they are not entitled, from a desire for revenge, to inflict punishment that cannot be justified on grounds of 'reparation and restraint'.[4]

The inconvenience of the state of nature is the presence of vicious and degenerate men whose evil actions bring into existence a state of war. In this state injustice is likely to be committed not only when the innocent are violated, but also when the wicked are subject to intemperate punishment by the innocent. Civil society is a rational construct designed to deter the wicked and to avoid their unjust punishment by providing 'a known authority to which every one of that society may appeal upon any injury received'.[5] This authority is the right of every man to punish transferred to the society as a whole. The right to life, liberty and property is retained by the individual. Indeed it is for 'the mutual preservation of their lives, liberties and estates'[6] that men entered into civil society. They have not consented to their being deprived of the gifts of God by an arbitrary decision on the part of any man. In a civil society the legislative assembly can go no further than to embody the law of nature in human law; a court can only pass impartial judgment where this law is broken and the executive can only protect the innocent and punish the guilty. In the event of a public official attempting to make, apply and enforce laws contrary to the law of nature the citizens as a body have the duty of resistance.

In barest outline this is the doctrine concerning the origin and form of legitimate government in Locke's *Second Treatise*, and it is either rooted in a theological doctrine or it is a radically incoherent one. If we are not to understand that man is God's servant there is no sense in which he may punish, as distinct from revenge himself, in the state of nature; for punishment, unlike revenge, is administered by authority. Even so, it can be argued against Locke, that given that it is in accordance with the law of nature that men punish they do not punish in accordance with a legal procedure, and that, therefore, until they enter civil society they take revenge on, rather than administer punishment to, those they deem offenders. Similarly, in a state of nature what Locke calls property on grounds of acquisition, cannot be distinguished from mere possession, for he does not explain how a man can have come to have legal title to it.

Locke's problem may be stated in another way. If civil society originates in a compact, in what sense is such an agreement binding if it is not binding in law enacted by a legislature, applied in a court and enforced by a state? And since legislatures, courts and kings characterize political society, and not the state of nature, it is difficult to see in what way the irreversible transition from the state of nature to civil society is effected. May not men who have simply agreed to form a civil society agree to dissolve their association, or, some, finding themselves in a minority on a political issue, refuse to accept the decision of the majority? If these are indeed flaws in Locke's argument it is puzzling that Locke did not see them. But are they really there?

If we take it that Locke seriously meant that men are the servants of their Creator, then they must surely stand in the same relationship to Him as do children to their father, i.e. subject to paternal authority. Locke admits the reality of paternal authority. His famous dispute with Filmer did not involve his denying paternal authority any more than the existence of God. It only involved a denial of the claim that human rulers have paternal authority over their adult subjects. We may conclude that, according to Locke, the right to legislate, apply and enforce law possessed by civil authorities has the same origin as the right of any adult and rational man to do what he honestly believes God would have him do, including the creation of civil society and the overthrow of tyranny. It is a divine right. What is then a right for Locke is a God-given right of one man against other men, and this inevitably entails a duty to God. The problem of men being able to punish, and hold property in a state of nature, and to enter civil society, arises only when we understand men to be free agents, rather than God's servants, and this Locke insists that they are not. Men may punish in accordance with God's command, hold property by his permission and form a civil society to fulfil His intentions, because God, unlike men, is purely rational and does not require rules to guide and bind Him. As the Supreme Being he may decree what is the appropriate conduct for those he has created. But, it may be objected, if this is the case, Locke's argument against Filmer is altogether less cogent than it first appeared. For is it not Filmer's argument that kings rule by divine right? It is, but the essence of Locke's case against Filmer is not that there is no such thing as a God-given right. It is the rejection of the claim that kings alone possess it. In Locke's view all rational men are equal in rights and equally the servants of their creator, and, if this makes human government nothing more than a trust, held on behalf of all of them, then so be it.

It cannot for a moment be entertained that Locke's political theory is perfectly consistent throughout, but when we take into account its theological base it has greater coherence than can otherwise be ascribed to it. Where Locke's theory can be said to present his admirers with serious difficulties these have more to do with his arguments being inconclusive than with their being inconsistent. His conclusions on the subjects of property, punishment and government may be compatible with his idea of God, natural law and the origin of civil society, but they do not necessarily follow from them to the exclusion of all other conclusions. It is possible to imagine alternatives. For example, if the right to punish can be said to have been institutionalized on account of the inconveniences which attend its exercise in a state of nature, then might not, in certain circumstances, the right to private property, as distinct from the possession of wealth, have been so transferred? Such circumstances might be said to have attended the exercise of the right to private property in a society where all available land is already under private ownership, and many willing to labour were excluded from the privilege of owning an estate. Locke's account of the origin of property does not necessarily sanctify the law of inheritance as it stood at the time of his writing his *Second Treatise*. It might well be used to establish a right to the product of one's labour, but not to the means of production. The means of production, particularly land, could be considered the property of the whole community. Once we admit the importance of empirical, as distinct from revealed, truth to the rationality of Locke's model of society, then this model owes as much to temporal as eternal circumstances. It seems to be an empirical fact that there were evil men in the state of nature as understood by Locke. Were this not a fact it would have been irrational for men to have formed a civil society. It is also a fact that there were a considerable number of propertyless men in England at the time Locke wrote his *Second Treatise*.

This kind of evasion of Locke's conclusions is not the only one that is likely to meet with success. In so far as Locke's political opinions are based upon his theological premises acceptance may be avoided by those who subscribe to different religions from the one Locke believed in, or by those who reject religion altogether. Locke could not reasonably expect to convince the conservative Catholic or atheist that he ought to accept the conclusions of the *Second Treatise* as valid. Theological arguments are forceful in political debate only when they are not themselves in dispute. By the time Mill came to write on the subject of representative government theology no longer carried the unquestionable authority it possessed in the seventeenth century. It is not surprising, therefore, that Mill sought to provide an alternative foundation for his political prescriptions.

J. S. Mill's Use of History in 'Considerations on Representative Government'

In his essay *Utilitarianism* Mill observes that 'the detailed doctrines of science are not usually deduced from, nor depend for their evidence upon, what are called first principles ... But though in science the particular truths precede the general theory, the contrary might be expected to be the case with a practical art, such as morals or legislation'.[7] Here a knowledge of the correct principles is indispensable to sound judgment. It is with a practical objective in view that Mill set out to present the 'philosophical grounds which can be given for assenting to the utilitarian standard . . .'[8] According to this standard 'actions are right in proportion as they tend to promote happiness, wrong as they tend to produce the reverse of happiness'.[9] Mill believes that it is possible to show that whatever men might affirm to be desirable, its desirability originated in the pleasure which accompanied the pursuit or attainment of it. And he suggests that it is 'quite compatible with the principle of utility to recognize the fact, that some kinds of pleasure are more desirable and more valuable than others'. It is, he informs us, 'better to be a human dissatisfied than a pig satisfied, better to be Socrates dissatisfied than a fool satisfied. And if the fool, or the pig, are of a different opinion, it is because they only know their own side of the question.'[10]

In *Considerations on Representative Government*, Mill argues that the best form of government is representative government, because this alone can guarantee the fullest development of the intellectual capacity, moral character and creative energy of every individual. In short, men ought to achieve the introduction of representative government, because this can best prepare them for the pursuit of the qualitatively superior pleasures of civilized life. Mill sets himself the task of demonstrating the superiority of representative government, and how those as yet unprepared for it may eventually possess it. To do so he presents what he considers to be the evidence of history. He tries to show that whenever any semblance of representative government has been established communities 'have both been more exempt from social injustice and crime, and have attained more brilliant prosperity, than any others, or than they themselves after they lost their freedom. Contrast . . . the Greek cities with the Persian Satrapies; the Italian republics and the free towns of Flanders and Germany, with the feudal monarchies of Europe, Switzerland, Holland and England, with Austria and ante-revolutionary France. Their superiority,' he claims, 'in good government and social relations is proved by their prosperity, and is manifest besides in every page of history.' [11] Where intellectually despotism has produced 'nothing better than the mystical metaphysics of the Pythagoreans or the Vedas', [12] the 'practice of the dicastery and the ecclesia raised the intellectual standard of the average Athenian citizen far beyond anything of which there is yet an example in any other mass of men, ancient or modern'. [13] In moral terms, according to Mill, where we find lethargy and envy has arrested the development of Latin people we find in the Anglo-Saxon race 'the best hopes for the general improvement of mankind'. [14] Why? Because 'the passive type of character is favoured by the government of one or a few, and the active self-helping type by that of the Many'. [15] History enables us to approve of despotism only where it imposed the discipline necessary for a people to take the first steps towards civilization. Such 'appears to have been the idea of the government of the Incas of Peru; and such was that of the Jesuits of Paraguay'. [16] In spirit they may be compared with the earliest rule of the Greeks and Jews in which we find 'the starting-point and main propelling agency of modern cultivation'. [17]

It is Mill's opinion that although democracy is the best form of government, it cannot be successfully established where a people have not reached the level of development at which they are willing to accept it, prepared to carry out the tasks which sustain it and able to assist it to achieve its objectives. Upon this rests the case for paternal government. At the time of writing Mill did not believe that everyone in England had reached the required standard, since he considered it desirable to exclude from the franchise those without a basic education and those who did not directly contribute to the Exchequer. Real democracy had to be distinguished from 'the falsely-called democracies which now prevail, and from which the current idea of democracy is exclusively derived'. [18] To protect real democracy against the domination of inferior intelligence, and the selfish interest of the numerically superior class, he proposes the introduction of proportional representation, and plural voting for the most educated sector of society.

In his preface to *Representative Government* Mill informs us that the work is based upon the principles to which he had subscribed for the greater part of his life. Because he makes this claim reference has been made to these principles as defined in *Utilitarianism*. Mill argues that happiness alone is good, but the pleasures of civilized men are superior to those of inferior cultural attainment. It follows, he believed, that the form of government which encourages the progress of civilization is the best one. In *Representative Government* Mill attempts, on the basis of historical evidence, to prove that a type of democracy is this form of government. Now to do this he would have to show, firstly, that under this democratic rule men have been happier than they would otherwise have been, and secondly, that it is the form of government that is responsible for making them happier. He does not do so. He confines his attention to an attempt to prove that democracy is conducive to progress, not happiness. Although he is able to provide some evidence that democracies have been inhabited by men whose achievements he admires, he provides none that they were happier than they would have been without the cultural achievements he admires. Nor could he properly hope to do so. Historical evidence might establish that Socrates was unhappy. It might establish that his unhappiness was unconnected with the fact that he lived in a democracy, good or bad, but it cannot establish that he was happier than a fool. This claim, from which is derived the prescriptive force of Mill's essay on representative government, rests on his opinion that all cultured men believe that the pleasures of the educated mind are superior to those of the uneducated person, and that they are not mistaken in this belief. Nothing else supports it.

Be this as it may, we might still ask, has Mill shown that democracy encourages progress? Has he proved that it is responsible for a higher level of intellectual, moral and material achievement amongst those subject to it than they could otherwise hope to attain? Again, the answer must be that he has not. He has not shown that it is democracy which has civilized man, and not civilized man who has democratized government. To show that representative government promotes increased human capacity requires something more than examples of human achievement and democratic government co-existing in time. It also requires an explanation as to why, for example, democracy and cultural achievement did not coincide during the Renaissance.

The purpose of Mill's venture into history is to go beyond illustration and achieve a comparative analysis of human experience with a view to elucidating the principles of cultural development. *Representative Government* marks a step away from history and philosophy towards sociology. History, for Mill, hardly enjoys an independent status as a discipline. However, Mill's step is but a tentative one. It is Herbert Spencer, rather than Mill, who chose to found his liberalism wholly on the findings of the new science of social evolution.

Spencer's Appeal to Sociology in ' The Man versus the State'

On the basis of a survey of liberal legislation, during the period 1860–83, Spencer concluded in *The Man versus the State* that liberals 'have lost sight of the truth that in past times liberalism habitually stood for individual freedom versus state-coercion'.[19] From a desire to mitigate human suffering they were now committed to a policy more in accordance with Tory than with their own principles properly conceived. It 'has happened that popular good has come to be sought by liberals, not as an end to be indirectly gained by relaxations of restraints, but as the end to be directly gained. And seeking to gain it directly, they have used methods intrinsically opposed to those originally used.' [20] Their mistake takes the form of a failure to associate policies with social structures. The benevolent intentions of liberals have blinded them to the fact that the positive promotion of human well-being by legislation must lead to despotism. To illuminate this startling error Spencer set out to define the nature of 'true' liberalism by contrasting two forms of social structure, the militant and the industrial.

In the militant society human relationships are determined by status. In the industrial form they are regulated by contract. Militant society is hierarchical and dependent on compulsion.

Industrial society is egalitarian and based on voluntary co-opera-tion. The former was defended by Tories and the latter by Whigs until recent times. The Whig conception of government involves no more than conditional obedience on the part of the individual. The citizen, in this view, is not obliged to obey the arbitrary commands of an absolute sovereign. Passive obedience is a Tory not a Whig doctrine. The Whigs had always resisted paternalism. Not so the modern liberal. Contrary to his heritage he has convinced himself that representative government, unlike monarchical rule, cannot invade the liberty of the citizen. He has failed to appreciate the fact that although legislation designed to protect the individual from industrial exploitation and urban squalor, disease and accident might prove popular, popular or not, it necessarily imposed coercive regulations on every member of society. And governments which take it upon themselves to direct human affairs are Tory in character. 'Standing as it does for coercion by the state versus the freedom of the individual, toryism remains toryism, whether it extends this coercion for selfish or unselfish reasons.' [21]

In Spencer's view the consequences of the error of modern liberalism are grave, for it involved a threat to the structure of industrial society, based as it is on contractual relationships. In order that children survive and learn to fend for themselves it is in accordance with nature that they be subject to parental direction. But it is equally in accordance with nature that grown men independently compete with one another for survival. Without parental protection infants must perish and the species become extinct. Without competition between men, merit will not receive its just reward. The inevitable result is falling productivity and starvation. The achievements of civilization are the product of struggle. Legislation which makes provision for the idle and unfit discourages it. This simple truth is not a new discovery. For example, the command '"if any would not work neither should he eat", is simply a Christian enunciation of the universal law of Nature under which life has reached its present height—the law that a creature not energetic enough to maintain itself must die: the sole difference being that the law which in the one case is to be artificially enforced, is, in the other case, a natural necessity'. [22]

The greatest affliction suffered by Victorian society is the ignorance of its legislators and electors. A Member of Parliament 'lately from college . . . fresh from keeping a pack of hounds . . . emerging from a provincial town . . . rising from the bar . . . does not know how little he knows, for the public at large agrees with him in thinking it needless that he should know anything more than what the debates on the proposed measures tell him'.[23] The disasters of 'unlimited law making' by men such as this are 'enormous . . . compared with . . . uninstructed medical treatment'.[24] Until politicians carry out 'a systematic study of natural causation as displayed amongst human beings socially aggregated', there can be no hope for progress.[25] 'Unquestionably among monstrous beliefs one of the most monstrous is that while for a simple handicraft such as shoe making, a long apprenticeship is needful, the sole thing which needs no apprenticeship is making a nation's laws!' [26]

Now according to Spencer, one of the consequences of this ignorance is the belief held by liberals that parliaments enjoy unlimited sovereignty. Did they but understand that political institutions have been formed with the sole purpose of protecting the rights of individuals they would not have concluded that majority decisions are absolutely binding on all. Just as the majority amongst the members of a book club cannot legitimately devote the club's funds to acquiring equipment for rifle practice so a majority of the members of a political society cannot rightly devote public revenue to the encouragement of idleness. A government, no matter how popular, cannot legitimately confer a right to public assistance on men unprepared to help themselves. Rights and duties are not the creation of law. They may only be recognized in law. Anthropological study has revealed that society has everywhere preceded the formation of government, and that human rights were first embodied in custom. These may properly be termed natural rights, since they have proved compatible with the laws of nature. Man's natural rights are those which facilitate the survival and progress of his species. It is in defence of these rights that men have co-operated in resisting external enemies and punishing criminals. Reasonable men have been prepared to abide by majority decisions only so long as they do not lead to the destruction of the conditions for their civilized life. Their 'subordination is not legitimate beyond this; since, implying as it does a greater aggression upon the individual than is requisite for protecting him, it involves a breach of the vital principle which is to be maintained'.[27] And this is: 'If each, having freedom to use his powers up to the bounds fixed by the like freedom of others, obtains from his fellow men as much for his service as they find them worth in comparison with the service of others ... then there is maintained ... individual life and social life. Further, there is maintained ... social progress, in as much as, under such conditions, the individuals of most worth will prosper and multiply more than those of less worth.' [28] The authority of all forms of government, when the purpose of government is properly understood, must be seen to be limited by 'an ethical sanction which, as we find, is desirable from the laws of human life as carried on under social conditions'.[29] Failure to recognize as much inevitably leads to undesirable consequences.

In *The Man versus the State* Spencer's central argument takes the following form: there is a universal law of nature prescribing the conditions for material progress as distinct from those for stagnation. In the past liberal policies were in conformity with this law, now they are not. They are, therefore, to be condemned as false liberalism. However, Spencer does not show that there exist laws of nature of the kind he defined. His 'laws of human life as carried on under social conditions' are merely biological metaphors. Spencer produces no evidence that they demonstrate the mechanism of social change in a way that might enable him to prove that the Victorians would have been better off without the kind of legislation of which he is critical. The sociological foundation Spencer constructed for liberalism is inadequate if only for the reason that its claim to be a scientific theory cannot be substantiated by his examples of its illuminating social development. His arguments have the form but not the substance of scientific ones. But this is not the main reason why they are inadequate. Even if the theory was genuinely scientific it could not be used to distinguish between true and false liberalism. The laws of nature are not the same as the principles of liberalism. Liberals are perfectly free to reject the idea of material progress at any price without violating the laws of nature. It is, in fact, quite impossible for a set of normative beliefs to conflict with an empirical hypothesis.

The Man versus the State did not turn the tide of liberal opinion against the kind of legislation to which Spencer was opposed, but this fact is, in all probability, unconnected with the book's logical failures. The new development in the relationship between the state and the subject had a life of its own. Far from being arrested by Spencer's writing it called for a new interpretation of the essence of liberalism. This was provided by T. H. Green.

T. H. Green's Philosophical Argument in 'Lectures on the Principles of Political Obligation'

Lord Lindsay's introduction to Green's *Lectures* states that the English Idealists, of whom Green was one, were 'convinced that utilitarianism had become barren as a political creed because of the inadequate philosophy upon which it was based, and that no further progress could be made in an understanding of politics till a new philosophic basis was found for liberalism'.[30] Lindsay frankly admitted that 'the practical success of a doctrine is no witness to its intellectual consistency',[31] but it is evident that he, like Green, believed that a coherent moral theory would lend support to cherished political beliefs. In the *Lectures* Green informs us that his 'purpose is to consider the moral function or object served by law, or by the system of rights and obligations which the state enforces, and in so doing to discover the true ground or justification for obedience to law'.[32] The question to which he addresses himself is not: What is political obligation? It is: Why and when should we obey the law? His objective is, as Lindsay perceived, a practical one. It is to find the operative criterion for distinguishing good from bad laws in the modern state, and for Green this is a moral principle.

According to Green, because our moral life involves the pursuit of self-perfection, every responsible member of society may be considered to have a right to pursue self-improvement. The business of law is the protection of the possibility of exercising this right. However, the law cannot enforce the exercise of the right, because the moral improvement of a man cannot be promoted by force. Man's character cannot be improved by his being compelled to do good. The good character is formed only by the willing of desirable action. However, Green's rejection of what he understood by paternalism did not entail his advocating laissez-faire. 'The true ground of objection to "paternal government",' he explicitly states, 'is not that it violates the "laissez-faire" principle and conceives that its office is to make people good, to promote morality, but that it rests on a misconception of morality. The real function of government being to maintain conditions of life in which morality shall be possible . . .' [33] The business of government is to guarantee the circumstances in which the citizen may exercise his right to participate in the pursuit of the common good. The rights of man which may be deduced from the fundamental right to be a moral person do not exist prior in time to the formation of society, and the claim to their possession may not be justified on utilitarian grounds. Their defence is possible only on the basis of their being a necessary prerequisite for the development of good character.

Green's view of the state is organic in the sense that he saw its evolution as inseparable from the evolution of man's moral consciousness. The state is, therefore, inseparable from the growth of society itself. The state simply 'secures and extends the exercise of powers, which men, [who] influenced in dealing with each other by an idea of common good, . . . had already in a certain measure secured to each other in consequence of that recognition. It is not a state unless it does so.' [34]

It is because the moral rules are social, and not legal, that respect for the rights of man does not entail a moral duty to obey all laws no matter what they prescribe. Laws 'may be inconsistent with the true end of the state as the sustainer and harmonizer of social relations'.[35] Civil disobedience, therefore, is permissible where it can be shown that it is 'contributory to some social good which the public conscience is capable of appreciating, not necessarily one which in the existing prevalence of private interests can obtain due acknowledgment, but still one of which men in their actions and language show themselves to be aware'.[36] But having said this Green felt obliged to admit that as a 'general rule, no doubt, even bad laws, laws representing the interest of classes or individuals as opposed to those of the community, should be obeyed. There can be no [moral] right to disobey them, even while their repeal is urged, on the ground that they violate rights, because the public interest, on which all rights are founded, is more concerned in the general obedience to law than in the exercise of those powers by individuals or classes which the objectionable laws unfairly withhold.' [37] It seems that the moral consciousness of government and society either develops as of a piece, in response to experience, or it must be left to rest at its existing level. In fact, the distinction between ideal and actual legal obligation made by Green would seem to have little utility. He cannot deny that both are equally obligations. This impression is confirmed when we turn to Green's application of his principle of moral and legal obligation to problems of conscience concerning war, punishment, property and marriage.

It is Green's opinion that the only acceptable justification for war, punishment, property and upholding the marriage contract is the maintenance of the social conditions for the moral development of individuals. It is also his opinion that the individual who would object to any one of these cannot carry his protest beyond stating his opinion unless he can be sure of the support of most of his fellows. When called upon by the state to fight in a popular, but unjust, war, this unhappy man is left to hope that one day 'the abatement of national jealousies and the removal of those deep-seated causes of war which, as we have seen, are connected with the deficient organization of states . . . may come to be realized'.[38] In the event of his witnessing unjust punishment he must 'wait till a system of rights has been established in which the claims of all men, as founded on their capacities for contributing to social well-being, are perfectly harmonized, and till experience has shown the degree and kind of terror with which men must be affected in order to (achieve) the suppression of the anti-social tendencies which might lead to the violation of such a system of rights'.[39] Still, the individual who believes that the unequal distribution of property originating in 'the arbitrary and violent manner in which rights over land have been acquired . . .'[40] might justifiably feel able to support a party committed to the appropriation, by the state, of unearned increment from such land. But Green cannot encourage this belief. Though 'fair enough in itself, the great objection is that the relation between earned and unearned increment is so complicated, that a system of appropriating the latter to the state could scarcely be established without lessening the stimulus to the individual to make the most of the land, and thus ultimately lessening its serviceableness to society'.[41] Finally we come to the implications of Green's principle of morality for the state's relationship to the family. As we might expect we are told that the 'ground for securing to individuals in respect to the marriage-tie certain powers as rights, is that in a general way they are necessary to the possibility of a morally good life, either directly to the persons exercising them or to their children'.[42] Now since adultery is damaging to this life we might conclude that it ought not merely to be a ground for divorce; it ought to be discouraged by punishment. Green accepts that adultery should be a ground for divorce, but not that it ought to be punishable. In his opinion the 'man in whom disloyal passion is neutralized by fear of punishment will contribute little to his family life, to the moral development of himself, his wife, or his children'.[43] Moreover, although Green accepts that there may exist such a degree of incompatibility of temper between the marriage partners, 'that with a view to the interests of the children, who ought in such a case to be chiefly considered, divorce implied less wrong than the maintenance of the marriage tie',[44] he does not agree that divorce should here be allowed. He is of the opinion that 'to hold out the possibility of divorce on the ground of incompatibility is just the way to generate that incompatibility'.[45] Well might we ask why, if the incompatibility of marriage partners may not be allowed as a ground for divorce, because it will encourage the complaint, allowing divorce on grounds of adultery may not be supposed to encourage this violation of the marriage relationship?

The question inevitably arises on a critical reading of Green: What, if anything, necessarily follows in terms of giving or withholding obedience to particular Victorian laws for the man accepting Green's theory of political obligation? The answer seems to be that nothing definite follows from holding Green's theory to be valid. Even if we admit that Green is right in basing the citizen's obligation to comply with the law on the expectation that it may, in the cases examined, provide the condition in which he will form a good character, we may still disagree with Green as to what constitutes a good character, and thereby avoid accepting the particular legal obligations he recognizes. It would be more direct, although less forceful, had Green entitled his lectures: 'A Non-Conformist's Liberal Principles of Political Obligation'. His audience would then have, more immediately, a clear idea of the origin of those beliefs for which he would present a lengthy rationalization.

Locke, Mill, Spencer and Green conceive the business of the political theorist to be the spelling out of the political implications of God's law, the principle of utility, the laws of nature and the logic of idealist obligation respectively. Their works on the form and purpose of good government are works of political education concerned to make, on the basis of universal principles, specific recommendations designed to influence conduct. In short, in order to communicate political convictions claimed to be more certain than those acquired in the ordinary course of political experience, they have appealed to one or more of the following disciplines: theology, history, science and philosophy. They are ideologists in search of a binding argument to convince the sceptical of the validity of their own convictions. It is evident from their arguments that they are each intent, one, on presenting a premise which is both indisputable and preferable to any alternative; two, demonstrating that their conclusions logically follow from their chosen premise and three, that there is no reason to believe that other conclusions might follow incompatible with those which they have drawn. Now whether or not it is possible to construct such an ideological argument it is difficult to say, but it is not difficult to show that Locke, Mill, Spencer and Green have failed to perform the task on behalf of liberalism. Locke did not demonstrate the truth of Protestant Christianity. He assumed it, and, having assumed it, he did not prove that it necessarily sanctified constitutional monarchy and the protection of private property as distributed in England at the time his *Second Treatise* was published. Mill's application of the principle of utility, his argument that democracy civilizes men and that civilized men are the happiest men are all far from being adequate. Spencer's laws of nature are neither scientific nor capable of serving as a criterion of political evaluation, and the logical relationship between Green's principles of moral obligation and his views on the desirable legal duties of his contemporaries is elusive. When it comes to telling their readers, whichever their case requires, what is in accordance with the will of God, the principle of utility, the laws of nature and the conditions of a moral life, Locke, Mill, Spencer and Green tell us what *they* happen to think will please God, make men happy, secure progress and make men moral, at the time of writing. They have found no alternative to stating their own beliefs; beliefs they acquired in the course of their everyday lives. The appeal they make to a-temporal and universal principles does not enable them to transcend the temporality and locality of this experience. Their opinions are historically relative. Their being relative, however, does not diminish the claim that they are liberal opinions. Moreover, their failure to show that particular political prescriptions necessarily follow from certain theological, historical, scientific or philosophical arguments does not refute the claim that the attempt to establish the connection is ideological. The claim that is invalidated is the claim that any one of these attempts establishes the form and content of the doctrine of true or real liberalism.

6 The Ideological Character of Liberalism

In the course of this study a number of methodological considerations relevant to writing about the ideological tradition of liberalism have been raised. A definite stand has been taken on the way in which the task might usefully be undertaken. Three approaches to the subject-matter have been rejected as necessarily misleading. The first to be dismissed affirms that liberalism consists in a particular set of political principles outlined by a leading exponent of its teaching. It has been argued that it is not possible to take the work of any one leading liberal theorist as presenting the paradigm example of liberal thought. Furthermore, it is not possible to select what appear to be the most prominent features of the teaching at this or that point in its evolution, or the most persistent features throughout its life, and maintain that these represent the essence of the doctrine. Each and every attempt to isolate what may be deemed to be the essence of liberalism results in the arbitrary rejection of the ideas of writers both claiming to be, and widely recognized as, liberals. The selection of what is taken to be genuine, or essential, liberal principles must itself be governed by the rule that they are to be found in the work of recognized liberals. Otherwise what is to be called the essence of liberalism will be a total invention. The exclusion of the ideas of other authors falling into the same category as those selected necessarily involves an inconsistency, and the portrayal of liberalism to emerge has to be defective. An accurate portrayal of the liberal tradition includes all the major points made by authors claiming to be liberals and recognized to be such by their fellow liberals, plus the points of authors subsequently recognized as the intellectual ancestors of liberal thinking by their descendants. It may no more exclude any of these points, because they are incompatible with others selected, than include points made by authors liberals have attacked, because they are compatible. Unless we are ourselves intending to make a contribution to the liberal tradition, we must resist the temptation to try and make of it a coherent theory of politics in spite of its many incompatible metaphysical foundations and conflicting policy recommendations.

The second claim to be rejected is that which suggests that there are a number of different kinds of liberalism found in different periods and countries. And so there would appear to be once we take a particular tenet of the liberal faith as being more than a particular application of a principle. Indeed, once we proceed in this direction we will find as many distinct kinds of liberalism as there are original liberal writers, if not distinct periods in their writing. The route leads straight to the same citadel of essentialism attacked by the first objection. A tradition of ideological writing does not possess, and is not in need of, the kind of coherence which an academic explanation requires. It may readily embrace incompatible principles and programmes. It is not an a-temporal understanding based on unalterable logic or evidence. It is an on-going evaluation of changing circumstances which may be said to admit a schism only when its adherents divide into camps engaged in a protracted dispute. Something like this came about for a period of time in Europe and America when liberal-conservatives and liberal-socialists argued over the role of the state. But the dispute was in no way confined by historical periods and national boundaries, and, although it paralleled the split in the English Liberal Party, it strengthened rather than weakened the liberal tradition of discourse. Liberalism displays a remarkable internationalism both in the respect its authors have accorded one another over four centuries in many countries, and in its persistent projection of an internationalist political programme. Liberalism is virtually unique amongst ideologies in that it is addressed to all men regardless of race, class, religion, nationality or language. It is addressed to every man in the world as an individual and nothing else. [11]

The third claim to be dismissed is related to the preceding two. It is the claim to have solved the problem of writing about a vision of political experience which has a certain form, but the face of which presents continually changing expressions to the world. It appears to have done so by taking the earliest complete expression of liberalism to be classical, and the rest to be a succession of revisions of this inheritance made in the light of new information. The temptation to adopt this approach has proved to be the one most seductive to liberal authors themselves. Because they have tended to regard liberalism as embodying the true principles of the best form of political practice they have conceived their own contribution to the tradition to be the correction of doctrinal errors exposed by the pursuit of unsuccessful policies wrongly supposed to be liberal. Errors of this kind, it is claimed, were made either by earlier liberal authors, who did not have the benefit of recent experience, or by recent ones, who would persist in supporting a policy, which once was progressive, but which is, in modern circumstances, positively harmful. However, as a tradition of ideological writing, liberalism cannot be presented as a set of claims about what qualities and skills are involved in the successful pursuit of good government, or what good government is like, some of which are true and others false. Liberalism sketches a picture of political experience; it is not a description of that experience. For example, the liberal and Marxist understanding of capitalism are not two different views of the same thing. Capitalism is two entirely different things in their view. It has always to be remembered that ideologists do not believe what they see, but see only part of the truth. They see all in the way of their belief and see all of what they believe.

Liberal works are intellectual projections based upon a view of the evolution of human potential and circumstances. They derive their significance from the context in which they make their appearance in the tradition of liberal thinking as a whole. Their significance is not derived from the relationship in which they stand to evidence of the kind that historians use to substantiate their claims about what happened in the dead past, or scientists to support their claims about what happens in the external world governed entirely by natural causes. In so far as the world is conceived in an ideology it is the particular world in which the adherents of this ideology live. It has no independent existence outside of the practical understanding prescribed. An ideology cannot be challenged by either facts or rival theories. In the case of liberalism all historical evidence is necessarily evidence for civilization, as characterized by liberals, having advanced or regressed. Every other ideology is a projection based upon a false understanding of human nature and man's past. Ideologists do make use of the findings of academic disciplines, but they confer on them a political significance which the methodology of those disciplines cannot confer. The ideologist cannot legitimately claim that his work derives authority from the methodology of any academic discipline. Advances in objective human understanding do not lead to advances in political thinking. The individual contributions to the liberal ideological tradition are each of them a new application of liberal principles. They are not the revision of false principles or a correction of the misapplication of true ones. Strictly speaking liberalism has not reached any conclusion about itself. Liberal authors have asserted this and that, but all of their ideological claims are open to rejection. The findings of science and history have always to be confirmed, but their confirmation properly conducted cannot be a matter of dispute. In ideological argument the only matter of fact is that, at this moment, we either do or do not agree. Nothing is settled for all, and once and for all, whether we all know it or not. The claim that liberalism has progressed is made by liberals and not by Marxists.

The negative findings of this study, then, are: one, that the essence of liberalism cannot be found in the work of a founding father, in the work of an author who wrote at what is deemed to be the pinnacle of its development, or in a position to reflect upon its whole past. Moreover, it is not to be distilled from the work of any number of leading liberal authors: two, that there are not a number of different kinds of liberalism which can be located in different periods of history and in different countries. The essences of liberalisms can no more be defined than can the essence of liberalism as a whole. And three, that liberalism is not a persistent and, at times, successful search for the true principles of politics, and that the first attempt to formulate these constitutes a classical inheritance which later liberal writers have revised in the light of new theories and facts. However, not all the findings of the study are negative. At least three are positive.

The first positive finding affirms that it is possible to distinguish liberal authors from the contributors to other ideological traditions on the basis of their historical reputation. This reputation has been claimed by men known as liberal, and it has been conferred on earlier writers who neither claimed to be liberal, nor were, during their lifetime, known as liberals. Once we have, on the basis of public reputation, discerned who are the authors and ancestors of liberalism, it is claimed that we may legitimately search for the limits which outline the identity of their work. The most important of these to be discovered constitute the symbolic form of the doctrine. It is said to be Newtonian, and it consists of three principles: the principle of balance, the principle of spontaneous generation and circulation and the principle of uniformity. For liberals, the good society is one in which different sections of the community and separate political institutions are counterbalanced to avoid the abuse associated with excessive accumulations of power, wealth and influence. It is one in which man's capacity for progress is realized through the creative power of the independent mind and the energy of the unintimidated will. According to liberals, the free circulation of ideas, private enterprise and the personal desire to do good can alone sustain the impetus of genuine civilization. This idea of civilization is one deemed to be of universal application wherever men are capable of appreciating its worth. These, the most prominent and persistent features of the liberal vision of experience, are called its symbolic form, because their symmetry is aesthetic rather than logical, and because the relationships they bear to the Newtonian conception of the universe is metaphorical. It is not claimed that there is anything scientific about this aspect of the doctrine. What is suggested is that the similarity between the symbolic form of liberalism and the Newtonian cosmology is significant to any consideration of possible reasons as to why liberalism has attracted adherents wherever European culture has taken root. They are both integral parts of that culture.

The second positive finding of the study is that the lasting appeal of many liberal conclusions originates in the power of a set of related arguments to convey this point of view with a vigour undiminished by their persistent and varied application. The adoption and amalgamation of these arguments, which have various origins, constitute the evolution of the liberal tradition of discourse. In Mill's essay *On Liberty* there are combined the argument brought forward during the Reformation to defend inviolability of conscience and that advanced by the English Whigs to draw a clear dividing line between matters rightly determined privately and those to be governed by public authority. These two arguments are integrated with those advanced by Renaissance scholars and Enlightenment thinkers which reject the authority of received opinion and justify freedom of learning and discussion as a condition of progress. Mill's famous distinction between self-regarding and other-regarding actions, and his equally famous plea for freedom of intellectual inquiry and the development of individual moral responsibility, are not his own invention. He gives them novel application when he uses them to attack the bureaucratic state and mass society, but they had been in circulation for some time previously. This fact is not unconnected with the immediate intelligibility of his essay to his Victorian readers, and the ring of authenticity it possessed for later liberals, no matter how critical they were of Mill's conclusions.

The third approach to understanding liberalism, which led to a positive finding, explores the logic of liberal arguments designed to prove that certain political prescriptions are founded upon incontestable metaphysical foundations, indisputable facts, verified hypotheses or necessary truths. However, it emerges that Locke's theological presuppositions, Mill's historical illustrations, Spencer's scientific analogies and Green's philosophical proofs fail to substantiate the claim that to evade their author's conclusions is irrational. At the same time, the examination of their arguments illuminates one of the characteristics of ideological writing—the urge to demonstrate a necessary connection between a theory and certain prescriptions and actions. The urge would appear to be particularly strong in the case of liberal thinkers. They believe that it is ideas, and not impersonal forces, which change the world, and see themselves as members of an intellectual élite whose self-appointed duty it is to do the people's thinking. They are all inclined to sympathize with the attitude expressed by Edward Beesly's contribution to *Why I am a Liberal: being Definitions and Personal Confessions of Faith by the Best Minds of the Liberal Party*, published in 1885.

> The right course in practical politics cannot be ascertained by mere reference to the will of the people at any given moment, but must be sought in conformity with the laws of order and progress revealed by the scientific study of man and his environment.[1]

By way of concluding this study of liberalism the sense in which it is an ideology is worth pursuing further. The attempt to relate theory to practice is not only a characteristic of ideological writing; the widespread belief that the attempt has been successful has had much to do with the passionate adherence to liberal and other political beliefs to be found in the modern world.

An ideological argument purports to present an objective view of human experience on the basis of which guidance is offered as to the correct form of future political conduct. The following quotations are presented to illuminate the ideological intention. They are taken from the introductions and in one case the conclusion to four post-war studies ostensibly dealing with the political implications of the findings of Christian theology, political philosophy, political science and the history of political ideas respectively. The first is the work of Geraint Vaughn Jones, the second of Friedrich Hayek, the third of Seymour Martin Lipset and the fourth of Karl Popper. All of them are liberals.

In his preface to *Democracy and Civilization*, Jones declares:

The matters dealt with are those involved in our contemporary civilization, including in particular democracy, which, I believe, is the chief hope for a reasonable organization of society incorporating, encouraging, and discriminating the values which approximate most closely to those implied in the New Testament and in the Christian conception of man and society, and for the lack of which the world has been plunged into disaster twice in a generation . . .[2]

In his introduction to *The Constitution of Liberty*, Hayek wrote:

As a statement of general principles, the book must deal mainly with basic issues of political philosophy, but it approaches more tangible problems as it proceeds . . . Our concern will be with the growth of an ideal, only dimly seen and imperfectly realized at most times, which still needs further clarification if it is to serve as a guide for the solution of the problem of our times.[3]

In the foreword and concluding chapter of *Political Man*, Lipset informs us:

A basic premise of this book is that democracy is not only or even primarily a means through which different groups can attain their ends or seek the good society; it is the good society itself in operation.[4]

This book's concern with making explicit the conditions of democratic order reflects my perhaps overrationalistic belief that a further understanding of the various conditions under which democracy has existed may help men to develop it where it does not now exist.[5]

And in his introduction to *The Open Society and its Enemies*, Popper tells us:

This book raises issues which may not be apparent from the table of contents.

It sketches some of the difficulties faced by our civilization—a civilization which might be perhaps described as aiming at humaneness and reasonableness, at equality and freedom; a civilization which is still in its infancy, as it were, and which continues to grow in spite of the fact that it has been so often betrayed by so many of the intellectual leaders of mankind. It attempts to show that this civilization has not yet fully recovered from the shock of its birth—the transition from the tribal or 'closed society' with its submission to magical forces, 'to the "open society" which sets free the critical powers of man'. It attempts to show that the shock of this transition is one of the factors that made possible the rise of those reactionary movements which have tried, and still try, to overthrow civilization and to return to tribalism. And it suggests that what we call nowadays totalitarianism belongs to a tradition which is just as old or just as young as our civilization itself. It tries thereby to contribute to our understanding of totalitarianism, and of the significance of the perennial fight against it.[6]

Clearly, the liberal scholars Jones, Hayek, Lipset and Popper believe, as do modern ideologists of all persuasions, that there exists a logical relationship between an objective understanding of observation and reflection and our capacity to give satisfactory shape to the course of events. In each case it is proposed to bring an academic discipline to bear upon a specific problem and in each case the problem is a practical one. They suggest that academic explanation can promote a prescription. The question we are now to consider is: can this be done? Can the liberal establish that there is a logical relationship between academic theory and political practice? The conclusion reached is that, except at the expense of coherent argument, the student of political theology cannot proceed beyond the theological significance of certain texts, the student of political philosophy beyond the philosophical significance of conceptual distinction and relation, the student of political science beyond the scientific significance of quantified comparison and the student of political history beyond the historical significance of the evidence for past thought and action. Nothing political emerges from their studies. In each case the academic's propositions are conceptually related at a particular level of abstraction. If the academic seeks to prescribe or justify action, while ostensibly dealing with meaning, form, occurrence or occasion, this involves a second level of abstraction which is, from the academic's standpoint, incompatible with the first. The academic and political understanding are distinct. The liberal ideologist may draw upon the academic's work for information of possible use in the world in which he lives, but he cannot, as an ideologist, explore the academic's understanding or establish its validity. The academic may make a study of ideology, but he cannot, as an academic, provide the support for the ideological conclusions others have reached. The pursuit of theoretical understanding with a view to persuading men that a course of action is desirable inevitably introduces a bias incompatible with the search for understanding for its own sake.

The theologian locates that which has a religious meaning in our experience. He is concerned with man's relationship to God, the form of good and evil, the significance of salvation and other aspects of religious teaching. To substantiate his conclusions he may properly appeal to revealed truth. The sacred text is as indispensable to him as the laboratory experiment to the scientist. Like the scientist he is concerned to establish that something is the case, not that something should be done. He is concerned to establish the significance and form of those aspects of experience which are eternal. He is not concerned to devise a way in which the Creation can be improved. He is concerned to explain why there is sin in the world, and in what it consists. Christians have the duty to resist sin, and the theologian is concerned with the status of this duty, but he is not concerned to prescribe that men resist sin. God has prescribed that they resist it. And, in so far as men are tempted to sin, God has ordained it, and it would be a gross presumption for the theologian to attempt to devise the abolition of sin in the way the liberal ideologist would abolish ignorance or the socialist exploitation. Those aspects of experience which interest the theologian are all of them unalterable.

The political philosopher may be understood as one who confines his attention to presenting the principles of an identifiable political experience in the form of a coherent and interdependent set of propositions. His object is to determine the logical form of an understanding of a practice. He lays bare the conceptual framework of an understanding of political experience. Experience which falls outside the structure the political philosopher has elaborated is set aside as a-political. It may, for example, be defined as moral, economic, industrial or religious, but it cannot here be understood to be political. Unlike the ideologist, the political philosopher, *qua* philosopher, has nothing to prescribe other than the logic, or a criticism, of an understanding of politics over a period of time and in a particular place. It would have been impossible for Plato to answer the question: What is Justice? if there is no possibility of the Greeks making consistent use of the term. Supposing, for example, the Greek word for justice were the same as their word for prudence: in so far as the use of the term would then be arbitrary, its meaning is obviously incapable of clarification by demonstrating distinctions and relations between applications of it and other Greek political terms. A linguistic usage that is in no sense concrete is not one that can have its limits determined at a particular time and place. It is not necessary that there be justice in the world before the philosopher can attempt to determine what, in a particular society, constitutes a just relationship, or that anybody use the term correctly, but it is necessary that the word justice has a logically appropriate application in given contexts. Political philosophy is dependent on the existence of unalterable universals and given particulars.

The political scientist is engaged in formulating hypotheses defining relationships between quantified factors which have always been found to enjoy concomitant relationships when a particular form of political experience has materialized. The basis of the scientific understanding of a 'political process' is an intellectual construction designed to reveal regularity in the behaviour of political phenomena. On the basis of evidence for this regularity the political scientist is able to classify the varieties of political life and speak of the condition for their past existence. In comparing one political situation with another he searches for uniform patterns of development, and, to the extent that his analysis is valid, it is possible for him to be familiar with the changes materializing in the structure of a given type of political order. In so doing he relies upon future events proving analogous to past events of the kind in question, but the evidence for his hypothesis is always drawn from the past. His creative achievement lies in the elaboration of a theory within the terms of which puzzles concerning the relationship of evidence to hypothesis to date can be resolved, or the hypothesis suffer a disconfirmation once and for all time. The scientist takes the world as he finds it. Nature's processes cannot be changed.

The historian of political practice or political ideas may be said to set out to explain how the world has been understood by men whose experience is different from his own. His work takes the form of a narrated account of past action and thought as we may now understand it to have been comprehended by identified persons whose practice and reflection it was. The basis of this appreciation, of what would otherwise be a lost significance, is an interpretation of respectable evidence in the present for certain successive states of consciousness which occurred in the past. The sequences are seen as a continuous unfolding of ideas each having a unique significance in the particular context of its original setting. The historian is not concerned as to whether or not this understanding was adequate in the light of his own education, and he is not concerned with the practical implications of past action, desirable or undesirable, for present or future generations. The historical past is autonomous, and the evidence for it is, while we have it, unalterable.

An academic theory dealing with an experience consists of information related within the conceptual framework of a distinct manner of thinking about phenomena. To the extent that a theory of this kind structures the relevant information in a consistent way it may be regarded as complete and coherent within its own terms. In contrast, a practice is a form of conduct concerned to modify the world in which we live. It is never more than an involvement in an unstable set of circumstances. It is essentially 'on-going'. It may be interrupted or abandoned, but it is never complete. It must, to retain its identity, maintain continuity in its development, but it cannot achieve the degree of consistency which characterizes the intellectual masterpiece. The practice of conducting laboratory experiments, for example, undergoes modification to utilize new instruments of observation. But the order of the events which constitute the experiments has not changed. It is, therefore, possible that the theories which confer significance on the fleeting changes the scientist has observed are immortal orders of universal application. Unless it can be shown that the theory cannot relate the relevant evidence to its propositions the theory survives. Further evidence or argument may call for a new theory, but this does not necessarily replace the old one. In the future, a new revelation of God's will, unprecedented scientific observation, the discovery of hitherto lost historical evidence and the logic of a new theory of knowledge may provide theologians, scientists, historians and philosophers, respectively, with the occasion for new reflections, but these will join rather than replace existing ones.

Intellectual orders, be they theological, scientific, philosophical or historical, are all potentially masterpieces of lasting importance. They are each concerned with the universal significance of experience conceived in a particular way. To criticize an intellectual order of this kind, within its own terms, is to commit oneself to the view that it is, and always was, inadequate. The immortality of a demonstration consists in its being a coherent work requiring no amendment. Quite the contrary is true of a practice. Its survival in a world of change depends upon its flexibility in adjusting to new circumstances, and its modification does not imply that it was always inadequate in its earlier form. In this respect, practice is distinct from academic theory, and the attempt to conduct a practice on the basis of knowing why something is the case, as distinct from what to do, when to do it and how, cannot succeed.

Now a theological, philosophical, scientific or historical work may differ from another of its kind, and it is understandable that its author prefer it to those of others; but, on academic grounds, he is not obliged to prefer it unless it is a demonstrably more coherent and comprehensive thesis than the alternatives. Moreover, since the academic is not obliged to take any action upon his academic understanding he is not necessarily compelled to choose between alternative works of equal explanatory power. In contrast, the ideologist must commit himself to a single view of the world and reject all others, even though he cannot, for all of us, specify a satisfactory criterion of choice. We may entertain any number of interpretations of experience, but we can live in only one form of political order, at any one time, and we cannot be indifferent to which this is. Unless the ideologist can locate those who share his disposition, enrich their vocabulary and inform their point of view, there is little hope that they will be able to effect the changes both desire. The failure of a class of person to reach what Marx called 'consciousness' will preclude the possibility of their achieving political success. And, unless it is possible that these men reasonably expect to live in the way they believe they ought to live, they cannot be placed under the obligation even to try to conduct their lives in the prescribed fashion.

To be a theologian, philosopher, scientist or historian does not entail our belonging to a group or promoting this or that kind of action. To be of a profession indicates what we can claim to know, not what we believe. But to agree with Mill is to be a liberal, and to agree with Marx is to be a socialist, and, as liberals or socialists, we ought to be prepared to substantiate our identities by allegiance and action. An ideologist has conviction and convictions are held rather than demonstrated. We can show that we hold them by action, but not that they are true. Nothing we can do to change the world can possibly substantiate a claim to possess genuine theological, philosophical, scientific or historical understanding. The findings of academic disciplines cannot be substantiated by human actions. We cannot live in the worlds of theology, philosophy, science and history. They are a-temporal. We can pray in the Christian manner, but we cannot worship in theology. We may have a problem of moral weakness, but we may not solve it with a moral philosophy. Apples may fall on our heads, but we do not feel gravity. And we can remember the past, but we cannot recall it *as* history. Academic knowledge is a way of understanding the world, it is not the result of being in the world. We can be without it.

Ideologies are more like a set of provocations and directions than substantiations. Their potency lies in their power to arouse and orientate the dormant and confused, not to prove some men right and others wrong. In so far as they establish that an experience can be evaluated in a particular way, they establish that it is possible to justify the course of action they recommend in the terms of their own vocabulary. But the ideologist who fails to persuade men to act in the manner he prescribes has not necessarily failed to explain himself. It is possible for us to understand what the liberal has to say and reject his conclusions on the grounds that we believe that there are good reasons for following another course of action. The provocation and orientation offered by the ideologist cannot compel us to adopt the cause he wishes to promote. It cannot oblige us to change our minds or show that our actions are unreasonable. If, for example, Marxism were a discipline and not an ideology, it would presumably be capable of explaining nineteenth-century economic, social and political experience to men living both at the time of its conception and at any subsequent time to date. However, although Marxism doubtless shed light on the course of events for Marx and his followers, it cannot be held to have afforded the same illumination for those who profess liberal and conservative convictions. If we reject the Marxist position, then it is apparent that we are not Marxists, but it is not apparent that we are not the adherents of another ideology. However, if we refuse to entertain an argument within a particular academic discipline we are not, on this occasion, a different kind of academic, we are not being academic at all. Historians, for example, do not even reject science, when they write history, but liberals do reject Marxism by professing liberalism. We can have the reputation of being both historian and scientist, and at any time. But we cannot ever be Marxists today and liberals tomorrow without being suspected of inconsistency. Conviction and knowledge are entirely different in kind. We turn to ideology more to be confirmed in the beliefs we have accepted in the course of life than from the desire to know more about experience.

As a picture of the world in which we live an ideology elaborates, from one point of view, the complete geography of human relationships as yet imperfectly known to us, and indicates how imperfections in the harmony of this order may be remedied by appropriate action. Since the world portrayed is one of constant change, an account of the manner in which its existing configuration came into being is a useful basis upon which to project the course which future events are likely to take. This is intended to be of interest to all those who are inclined to identify themselves with the members of the society, class, nation or race specifically involved, since it is their lives that are to be affected in the manner projected. The purpose of the picture is to rouse the resolve to act by focusing attention on certain dangers threatening a way of life to which people are already committed, and by pointing out certain possibilities for improving it. It also provides the appropriate conceptual framework and vocabulary for the articulation of the relevant political judgment and the communication of relevant experience between like-minded adherents. Without this equipment it is doubtful that the kind of enthusiasm and co-ordination necessary to set a political movement in motion could be sustained and directed. In providing it liberal ideologists have been remarkably successful. An ideological understanding of the world is not objective in any academic sense, but it is not a random collection of ideas. Although all that is understood ideologically is understood within its own terms, without any external referent, any one ideological judgment is taken to be appropriate which either concurs with another, or is seen to be compatible with another, in the sense that it bears to it no incongruous relationship. For any two adherents of an ideology to be sure that they are right, it is enough that their points of view coincide. Ostensibly they are committed only to acting in the world, and, in deciding what to do and how to try and do it, agreement is sufficient.

A political ideology is intended, via action, to establish the identity of a body of persons who are thereafter to be understood to be related to one another in a particular way. The relationship is only one amongst many that each of the potential members of this group may, at a given time, have with a number of other persons, but it is the only relationship which ought, according to the ideology, to embrace them all. It has been claimed to be familial, commercial, tribal, racial, national, religious, civil or one of class. The business of the ideologist is to accentuate the value of a particular human relationship with a view to extending the size and increasing the cohesion of the group to whom he addresses his work. Without commitment the group cannot hope to transform its circumstances with a view to eliminating or isolating relationships incompatible with the one deemed to be ideologically sound. (One thinks of the Nazi Party's appeal to German youth to place allegiance to the Aryan race above that to family and report parental impropriety to party officials.) To encourage the desired consciousness the ideologist offers an interpretation of the past, and a projection of the future, based upon a prejudicial assessment of the present. Although he claims that this understanding represents the reality behind the appearance of things at any time this has to be illegitimate. We cannot, on the basis of human experience, have definitive knowledge about the present—the condition of being now but never being now for any length of time. The experience of which the ideologist speaks is always incomplete. It is an experience in the making. It is the experience of acting, not the business of reflecting on a given experience. For the ideologist what our past and future may be understood to be is to be determined here and now, but it is not as yet determined. The ideological understanding does not call for analysis, it calls for assertion, and to the extent that the adherents of an ideology assert themselves the more difficult will it be for others to counter their action. The ideologically orientated are intent on turning society inside out so that an unfinished work will be made complete and others are destroyed beyond repair. It is an attempt to authorize the creation of a coherent way of life. It would seem that coherence is the ideologist's dream. However, it seems that it is a dream that cannot be realized in so far as it requires putting an ideological theory based upon academic understanding into practice.

Theology, philosophy, science and history all refer to what can be identified as a given experience. Theology cannot proceed beyond what has been revealed by God. Philosophy can go no further than to show the logic of a possible understanding. Science cannot contradict the findings of laboratory experiments and history cannot ignore the evidence for the way in which the determined past was understood when, as the then present, it was indeterminate and influenceable. Theology cannot invent or prescribe the divine purpose; philosophy cannot legislate what words do or ought to mean: science cannot influence the processes of nature or determine the condition under which men will live in a better world, and history cannot change the past or tell us what goals we should now be pursuing in life. Their claim to objectivity precludes the possibility of their attempting to do so. Ideologies which claim to establish the real meaning of words like liberty, equality and justice, the conditions for the good life and the form of the good life on the basis of theological, philosophical, scientific and historical research respectively are incoherent.

The modern ideologist is the intellectual grandchild of the sixteenth- and seventeenth-century theorist who founded his argument in theology in the belief that the cogency of his reasoning would then require that men follow the prescriptions to which it leads. It is only when men abide by the conclusions of his argument that there will be no experience demonstrably incompatible with the claims he makes. Naturally until such time arrives ideological arguments, which are orientated by a preference for a particular form of human relationship, are likely to be controversial. Every notable ideologist has written under the threat of another doctrine defending or advocating a different order. Calvin and Hooker, Filmer and Locke, Burke and Paine, Blackstone and Bentham, Mill and Maine, Marx and Hitler all put pen to paper on the subject of politics with a view to countering an alternative teaching. They each attempted to counter another argument prescribing a different programme to the particular one each individually believed would benefit mankind. However, because there is no way in which their intellectual claims can be supported, there is no way in which their incommensurability can be resolved. One ideological argument cannot refute another. It can do no more than provide a rebuttal. Ideological conflicts are confrontations of incompatible views. They are not, strictly speaking, debates on disagreements, because there are no procedures or criteria by which their differences can be settled by authority, evidence or rational argument. The polemical battles they promote are a prelude to war. It is to a tradition of ideological polemic that the liberal apostles of light and enemies of darkness, Jones, Hayek, Lipset and Popper, belong. Their attacks are dramatic rather than academic. To read and understand them in their authors' terms is to be caught up in the struggle they portray. They are invitations to participate in the conflict their authors would have us believe can be carried to a final and successful conclusion in the world. The struggle for the control of man's political inclination is a drama in which the audience is to play the decisive part. The ideologist succeeds to the extent that his reader finds himself prepared to make the sacrifices necessary to act out the part the ideologist has to assign to him in real life. Ideologists locate rather than convert those who come to be their adherents. In contrast, theology, philosophy, science and history can change minds, but they are incapable of calling for action. They refer to what is, not what ought to or may be. The price the academic must pay for being able to demonstrate the intellectual precision of his explanations is political impotence. He can say no more to those who find ideological argument distressing than could de Gaulle, who, in a rare liberal mood, said to his wife as they flew over Africa and she had just complained that she had seen elephants making love below: 'Laisse les faire'—'Let them be'.

Notes

1. The Symbolic Form of Liberalism

1. J. S. Mill, *Essays on Politics and Culture*, ed. Himmelfarb, New York 1963, intro., pp. viii–xvi.
2. *Liberalism*, New York and London 1964 (first published 1911).
3. *Studies in Philosophy, Politics and Economics*, Chicago and London 1967, p. 95.
4. *Readings from Liberal Writers*, London 1965, intro. p. 13.
5. *Two Treatises of Government*, ed. Laslett, Cambridge 1967, and New York 1960, *Second Treatise*, p. 58.
6. Ibid., p. 137.
7. Montesquieu, *The Spirit of the Laws*, ed. Newman, New York 1962, p. 150.
8. Barker, *Principles of Social and Political Theory*, London and New York 1951, p. 145.
9. *The Limits of State Action*, ed. Burrow, Cambridge 1969, p. 52.
10. *Lectures on Political Obligations, Works*, ed. Nettleship, New York 1968 (repr. of 1889 edn), Vol. II. pp. 39–40.
11. *Liberalism*, op. cit., p. 137.
12. *On Liberty*, ed. McCallum, Oxford 1948, p. 4.
13. Quoted in *Readings from Liberal Writers*, op. cit., p. 209.
14. *The Revolt of the Masses*, New York 1932, pp. 83–4.
15. *Liberal Legislation and Freedom of Contract, Works*, op. cit., Vol. III, p. 388.
16. *Representative Government*, ed. McCallum, Oxford 1948, p. 129.
17. Ibid., p. 141.
18. *Les Causes de la grandeur et de la decadence des Romains.* Quoted in Aron, *Democracy and Totalitarianism*, London 1968, p. 96.
19. *The History of European Liberalism*, London 1927, p. 362.
20. *Political Man*, New York 1959, and London 1960, p. 417.

21. *Representative Government*, Everyman Edition, London and New York 1972, p. 197.
22. 'Spirit of the Age', in *Essays on Politics and Culture*, ed. Himmelfarb, New York 1963, p. 43.
23. 'Thoughts on Parliamentary Reform', in *Essays on Politics and Culture*, op. cit., p. 320.
24. *Democracy in America*, ed. Heffner, New York 1961, p. 157.
25. *Works*, op. cit., Vol. III, p. 370.
26. Bronowski, *The Identity of Man*, New York 1971, p. 123.
27. *The Structure of Scientific Revolutions*, Chicago 1962, and London 1970, p. 92.

2. Liberty and the Liberal Tradition of Discourse

1. *Utopia*, intro. Warrington, Everyman's Library, p. 119.
2. Ibid., pp. 119–20.
3. *Works*, Leyden 1702, Letters, Appendix dcxxi.
4. Ibid.
5. *The Work of Mr Richard Hooker*, ed. Walton, Oxford 1841, Vol. II, p. 551.
6. *Leviathan*, ed. Oakeshott, Oxford 1960, and New York 1968, p. 360.
7. *Works*, trans. Elwes, New York and London 1951, Vol. I, p. 245.
8. Ibid., p. 259.
9. Ibid., p. 257.
10. *Leviathan*, op. cit., p. 327.
11. Ibid.
12. *The Prose Works of John Milton*, London 1833, p. 413.
13. Ibid., p. 417.
14. Ibid., p. 418.
15. *A Letter Concerning Toleration*, ed. Gough, Oxford and New York 1958, p. 125.
16. Ibid., pp. 127–8.
17. Ibid., p. 129.
18. Ibid., p. 143.
19. Ibid., p. 131.
20. Ibid., p. 132.
21. Ibid., p. 134.
22. Ibid., p. 150.
23. Ibid., p. 152.

24. Ibid., p. 153.
25. Ibid., pp. 157–8.
26. *Works,* London 1814, Vol. II, Book 6, p. 325.
27. Ibid., pp. 325–6.
28. Ibid., p. 335.
29. *The Philosophical Work of Francis Bacon,* ed. Ellis and Spedding, London 1905, p. 286.
30. Ibid.
31. *Discourse on Method,* Everyman's Library, p. 49.
32. *Theologico Politicus Treatise,* p. 261.
33. *Works,* op. cit., p. 108.
34. Ibid., p. 110.
35. Ibid., p. 113.
36. Ibid., p. 117.
37. *A Treatise on Toleration,* trans. Williams, London 1774, p. 26.
38. 'Essay on Toleration' in *The Works of Voltaire,* trans. Smollett and Francklin, London 1761–4, Vol. XVII, p. 115.
39. Ibid., p. 126.
40. Ibid.
41. *A Treatise on Man,* trans. Hopper, London 1777, Vol. I, p. 159.
42. *Enquiry Concerning Political Justice,* ed. Codell Carter, London and New York 1971, p. 226.
43. Ibid., p. 143.
44. Bentham Manuscripts, UCL Box 15, Folder 17, p. 542.
45. 'Liberty of the Press', reprinted from the Supplement to the *Encyclopaedia Britannica,* London 1821, p. 23.
46. *On Liberty,* Everyman Edition, London and New York 1972, p. 67.
47. Ibid.
48. Ibid., p. 68.
49. Ibid., pp. 167–70.
50. Ibid., p. 71.
51. Ibid., p. 75.
52. Ibid., p. 73.
53. Ibid., p. 73.
54. Ibid., p. 82.
55. Ibid., p. 83.
56. Ibid., p. 95.
57. Ibid., p. 96.

Liberalism

58. Ibid., pp. 116–17.
59. Ibid., p. 117.
60. Ibid., p. 170.
61. Ibid., p. 74.
62. *Liberty*, London 1930, Preface p. ix.

3. *The Unity of Liberal Ideology*

1. *Freedom: A New Analysis*, London 1953, p. 47.
2. Ibid., p. 65.
3. Ibid., p. 69.
4. *The Political Theory of Possessive Individualism*, London 1962, p. 269.
5. *Vindiciae Contra Tyrannos*, ed. Laski, London 1924, p. 96.
6. Ibid., p. 170.
7. *De Jure Belli ac Libri Tres*, ed. Fessey, London and New York 1925, Vol. II, p. 44.
8. *De Juri Natural et Gentium*, trans. Oldfather, London 1934, Vol. II, pp. 974–5.
9. *The Prose Works of John Milton*, op. cit., p. 231.
10. Ibid., p. 233.
11. *Two Treatises of Government*, op. cit., p. 159.
12. *Discourses Concerning Government*, Hamilton and Balfour, 1750, Vol. I, p. 103.
13. *Two Treatises*, op. cit. pp. 418–19.
14. *Discourses*, op. cit. p. 48.
15. Ibid., p. 302.
16. *The Works of Voltaire*, op. cit., Vol. XVII, pp. 69–70.
17. *Writings on Philosophy, Science and Politics*, ed. Passmore, New York 1965, p. 193.
18. *The Constitution of England*, London 1777, p. 58.
19. *The Spirit of the Laws*, op. cit., p. 1.
20. Ibid., p. 150.
21. Priestley's *Writings*, op. cit., pp. 187–8.
22. Ibid., p. 200.
23. *The Federalist Papers*, New York 1961, p. 301.
24. Ibid., p. 324.
25. *The Theory of Moral Sentiments*, London 1790, p. 235.
26. Ibid.

162

27. Ibid., p. 127.
28. Ibid., p. 343.
29. Ibid., p. 125.
30. Ibid., p. 331.
31. *An Inquiry into the Nature and Causes of The Wealth of Nations*, Aberdeen 1844, p. 354.
32. *The Political Works of Thomas Paine*, Chicago 1879, p. 17.
33. *The Works of Jeremy Bentham*, ed. Bowring. Edinburgh 1843, Vol. IX, p. 110.
34. *The Science of Rights*, trans. Kroeger, London 1970, p. 160.
35. *The Metaphysical Elements of Justice*, trans. Ladd, New York 1956, p. 47.
36. Ibid., p. 35.
37. Ibid., p. 81.

4. *The Dialectic of Liberal Doctrine*

1. The suggestion that an ideology is an abridgment of experience appears in M. J. Oakeshott's *Rationalism in Politics*, London and New York 1962.
2. *What is the Third Estate?* Ed. Finer, London 1963, p. 171.
3. *Considerations on the Principal Events of the French Revolution*, London 1818, Vol. II, p. 114.
4. Ibid.
5. *On the Political Doctrine calculated to Unite Parties in France*, trans. Darby, London 1817, p. 18.
6. 'Principles of Politics 1815' in *Readings from Liberal Writers*, op. cit., p. 212.
7. *Democracy and its Mission*, London 1848, p. 39.
8. *Democracy in America*, New York 1956, p. 32.
9. Ibid., pp. 137–8.
10. Ibid., p. 54.
11. Ibid., p. 148.
12. Ibid., p. 255.
13. Mill's review of *Democracy in America* in *Essays on Politics and Culture*, op. cit., p. 267.
14. 'The Convention of Cintra' in *The Political Tracts of Wordsworth, Coleridge and Shelley*, ed. White, London 1953, p. 139.
15. 'A Philosophical View of Reform' in *The Political Tracts of Wordsworth, Coleridge and Shelley*, op. cit., p. 211.

16. *The Duties of Man and Other Essays*, ed. Jones, Everyman's Library, p. 78.

17. Ibid., p. 50.

18. *Considerations on Representative Government*, Everyman's Library, London 1972, p. 362.

19. 'Nationality', in *History of Freedom and Other Essays*, London 1969, p. 288.

20. Ibid., p. 298.

21. *On the Limits of State Action*, ed. Burrow, London 1969, p. 16.

22. Ibid., p. 24.

23. Quoted in *Free Trade and Other Fundamental Doctrines of the Manchester School*, ed. Hirst, London 1903, p. xii.

24. 'The Classes of Labour', in *Dissertations and Discussions*, London 1859, Vol. II, p. 217.

25. *The Man Versus the State*, ed. Macrae, London 1969, p. 144.

26. *War and Other Essays*, New Haven, Conn. and London 1911, Vol. I, p. 117.

27. Ibid., p. 252.

28. *The Limits of Individual Liberty*, London 1885, p. 2.

29. Ibid.

30. Ibid.

31. Ibid., p. 35.

32. Ibid., pp. 186–7.

33. Ibid., p. 174.

34. *Lectures on the Principles of Political Obligation*, London 1963, pp. 32–3.

35. *Liberalism*, op. cit., p. 65.

36. Ibid., p. 66.

37. Ibid., p. 78.

38. *Principles of Social and Political Theory*, London and New York 1951, p. 268.

39. *Essays in Persuasion*, London and New York 1931, pp. 337–8.

40. *Individualism Old and New*, Allen and Unwin, London 1931, p. 21.

41. Ibid.

42. *Capitalism, Socialism and Democracy*, Allen and Unwin, London 1961, and New York 1962, p. 133.

43. Ibid., pp. 141–2.

44. *The Affluent Society*, London and New York 1958, p. 2.

45. *The Faith of a Liberal*, New York 1946, pp. 464–6.

46. *Politics and Morals*, London 1946, p. 106.
47. *The English Constitution*, London and New York 1963, p. 277.
48. *Popular Government*, London 1886, p. 158.
49. Ibid., p. 53.
50. *Democracy in Europe*, London 1877, intro. pp. lxv–lxvi.
51. *First Principles in Politics*, London 1899, p. 227.
52. *Democracy and Liberty*, London 1896, Vol. I, p. 227.
53. Ibid., pp. 21–2.
54. *The History of European Liberalism*, London 1927, p. 376.
55. *Liberty*, op. cit., p. 307.
56. *The Revolt of the Masses*, London 1969, p. 92.
57. *Liberty and Tyranny*, London 1935, p. 9.
58. Ibid., p. 40.
59. *The Good Society*, London 1938, p. 51.
60. *My Philosophy*, trans. Carritt, London 1949, p. 76.
61. *The Road to Serfdom*, London and Chicago 1944, p. 159.
62. Ibid., p. 148.
63. Ibid., p. 178.
64. *The Open Society and Its Enemies*, London and Princeton 1962, Vol. II, p. 280.
65. *On Power*, London and New York 1962, p. 257 (first published 1945).
66. *The Origins of Totalitarian Democracy*, London and New York 1961, p. 6.
67. 'Two Concepts of Liberty' in *Four Essays on Liberty*, New York 1968, and London 1969, p. 148 (first published 1958).
68. *Modern Democracies*, London 1921, Vol. I, p. 66.
69. *The Faith of a Liberal*, London 1933, pp. 12–23.
70. *Democracy in Europe*, London 1877, Vol. I, pp. xxvi–xxvii.
71. Ibid., p. lxiv.
72. 'Principle, Ideal and Theory of Liberty' (1939), in *Philosophy, Poetry and History*, trans. Sprigge, London and New York 1966, p. 720.
73. *Justice*, New York 1971, and London 1973.
74. *The Vocabulary of Politics*, Harmondsworth and New York 1953.

5. *The Foundations and Logic of Liberal Arguments*

1. *Two Treatises of Government*, op. cit., p. 289.
2. Ibid., p. 368.
3. Ibid., pp. 336–7.

4. Ibid., p. 290.
5. Ibid., p. 344.
6. Ibid., p. 368.
7. *Utilitarianism, Liberty, Representative Government*, Everyman's Library, London 1972, pp. 1–2.
8. *Utilitarianism*, op. cit., p. 5.
9. Ibid., p. 6.
10. Ibid., p. 9.
11. Ibid., p. 210.
12. Ibid., p. 212.
13. Ibid., p. 216.
14. Ibid., p. 214.
15. Ibid., p. 215.
16. Ibid., p. 199.
17. Ibid., p. 201.
18. Ibid., p. 276.
19. *The Man versus the State*, ed. Macrae, Harmondsworth 1969, p. 67.
20. Ibid., p. 70.
21. Ibid., p. 80.
22. Ibid., p. 83.
23. Ibid., p. 116.
24. Ibid.
25. Ibid., p. 132.
26. Ibid., p. 148.
27. Ibid., p. 179.
28. Ibid., p. 181.
29. Ibid., p. 183.
30. *Lectures on the Principles of Political Obligation*, London 1941, intro. p. vii.
31. Ibid., p. x.
32. Ibid., p. 29.
33. Ibid., pp. 39–40.
34. Ibid., p. 138.
35. Ibid., p. 148.
36. Ibid., p. 149.
37. Ibid., p. 150.
38. Ibid., p. 179.

39. Ibid., p. 189.
40. Ibid., p. 228.
41. Ibid., p. 229.
42. Ibid., p. 242.
43. Ibid., p. 240.
44. Ibid., pp. 242–3.
45. Ibid., p. 243.

6. *The Ideological Character of Liberalism*

1. *Why I am a Liberal*, London 1885, p. 21.
2. *Democracy and Civilization*, London 1946, p. 9.
3. *The Constitution of Liberty*, London and Chicago 1960, intro. p. 5.
4. *Political Man*, op. cit., p. 403.
5. Ibid., p. 417.
6. *The Open Society and its Enemies*, op. cit., intro. p. 1.

Select Bibliography

A. BULLOCK and M. SHOCK (eds), *The Liberal Tradition: From Fox to Keynes,* London and New York (O.U.P.), 1967.

T. D. CAMPBELL, *Adam Smith's Science of Morals,* London (Allen & Unwin) and Totowa, N. J. (Rowman & Littlefield), 1971.

I. COLLINS, *Liberalism in Nineteenth-Century Europe,* London (The Historical Association), 1957.

M. COWLING, *Mill and Liberalism,* London (C.U.P.), 1963.

J. DUNN, *The Political Thought of John Locke,* London and New York (C.U.P.), 1969.

G. E. FASNACHT, *Acton's Political Philosophy,* London (Hollis and Carter), 1952.

J. H. HALLOWELL, *The Decline of Liberalism as an Ideology,* London (Kegan Paul), 1946.

L. HARTZ, *The Liberal Tradition in America,* New York (Harcourt Brace), 1955.

L. T. HOBHOUSE, *Liberalism,* New York (O.U.P.), 1964.

S. R. LETWIN, *The Pursuit of Certainty,* London and New York (C.U.P.), 1965.

J. LIVELY, *The Social and Political Thought of Alexis de Tocqueville,* London (O.U.P.), 1962.

A. MACINTYRE, *Against the Self-Images of the Age: Essays on Ideology and Philosophy,* London (Duckworth) and New York (Schocken), 1971.

K. MINOGUE, *The Liberal Mind,* London (Methuen), 1963.

J. G. MURPHY, *Kant: the Philosophy of Right,* London (Macmillan) and New York (St. Martins), 1970.

M. J. OAKESHOTT, *Rationalism in Politics,* London (Methuen), 1962, and New York (Barnes & Noble), 1974.

J. E. OWEN, *L. T. Hobhouse, Sociologist,* London (Nelson), 1974, and Ohio (University Press), 1975.

L. PANGLE, *Montesquieu's Philosophy of Liberalism,* Chicago (University Press), 1973.

169

J. D. Y. PEEL, *Herbert Spencer: the Evolution of a Sociologist*, London (Heinemann) and New York (Basic), 1971.

J. PLAMENATZ, *Readings from Liberal Writers*, London (Allen & Unwin), 1965.

J. G. A. POCOCK, *Politics, Language and Time*, New York (Atheneum), 1971, and London (Methuen), 1972.

G. DE RUGGIERO, *The History of European Liberalism*, trans. R. C. Collingwood, London (O.U.P.) and Gloucester, Mass. (Peter Smith), 1927.

M. SALVADORI (ed.), *European Liberalism*, New York (Wiley), 1972.

J. S. SCHAPIRO, *Liberalism: Its Meaning and History*, New York (Van Nostrand Reinhold), 1958.

W. G. SUMNER, *Social Darwinism*, Englewood Cliffs, N. J. (Prentice-Hall), 1963.

T. D. WELDON, *The Vocabulary of Politics*, New York (Johnson Reproductions), 1971.

S. WOLIN, *Politics and Vision*, New York (Little, Brown), 1960.

Index